Stuff Your Fanny Pack With Coping Skills

FOR THE PERSON ON THE GO

Patricia I. Tilley, LMHC

Dedication

This book is dedicated in memory of my beloved mother, Madeline, whom I dearly loved. You were the best mom I could have ever asked for. Thank you for leaving me a legacy of faith.

The world changes from year to year,
our lives from day to day, but
the love and memory of you,
shall never pass away.

www.all-greatquotes.com

Acknowledgments

I am incredibly grateful that my Lord and Savior Jesus Christ believed in me to give me the task of writing this very important book on skills for those having general life challenges and those with mental health concerns. I have spent many hours praying and seeking the Lord's wisdom for what was needed to encourage and benefit those who could use coping skills to gain momentum to get out of the pit, forge through daily quandaries to keep on their wellness path, and then be sustained for a continued, forever life of wholeness and happiness. Those who are already professionals in the field will benefit from the unique stories and skills offered that their client can use in conjunction with the skills given by their therapist.

I am truly beholden to the talented and amazing team at Trilogy Publishing, who said yes to my manuscript and then so expertly made it all look so grand. Thank you for trusting me to give honor to this product.

Thank you to my three wonderful sons, David, Steven, and Michael, who were so exceptionally generous in contributing to my need so I could begin this dream of writing and helping others more fully. It has been a blessing that my husband, Jim, held down the home front, doing almost everything around here so I could spend time researching and writing. My remarkable friends and other exceptional family have given me encouraging words and prayer support for this endeavor that they regarded as something that would be very valuable to others. A special thanks to my sister-in-law, Sharon, who bought me a laptop so I could type on something new instead of the dinosaur desktop that kept messing up. Thanks to my son, Michael, who has the expertise and willingness to come to my rescue every time I have technical issues. Much thanks and love to you all.

Table of Contents

Preface

The idea for the book *Stuff Your Fanny Pack* came to me because mental health coping skills are so very much needed. Now more than ever people are more open to talking about their life challenges. As a licensed mental health counselor, I have used mental health coping skills for various populations, such as children and teenagers who were having difficulty with multiple issues with school, families, and with their personal depression, anger, fear, and self-confidence. For many years I counseled and facilitated groups for adults who battled with a host of life problems in their marriages, family life, and predominately with their disappointments, stress, worry, loneliness, and finding their purpose. I am a veteran and worked with veterans on resiliency, anxiety, negative thinking, and regrets.

This book is very comprehensive, covering seventeen main challenge areas as just mentioned, and within each of those categories, there are eighty-four additional insights. Each chapter has an educational piece, quotes, or stories to help the concept come alive and be interesting. There are over 500 coping skills in the book, which is basically unheard of to be that extensive. Every page has a pertinent scripture because, in addition to the practical aids, "my help comes from the Lord" (Psalm 121:2, NIV).

The name fanny pack came by inspiration along with the insight of my daughter-in-law, Meagan, who loves fanny packs. She reports, "I wear mine everywhere like a purse, and I put my phone, wallet, and keys in it." Fanny packs are unisex and can have a manly vibe to them when worn across the chest. They are very accessible, and your valuables are kept near and safe. Therefore, when we need a coping skill, the symbolism is it is right with us:

useful, comfortable, and even fashionable. Since life is unpredictable, we need skills that are practical, bring us comfort, and are cutting edge. So read on and stuff your fanny pack!

Introduction

And so your journey begins through this book. "Journey" means "passage from one place to another." It comes from the words *la journee*, which mean "by day." It is my expectation that your journey through these seventeen mental health categories, eighty-four subhead subjects, and over 500 coping skills will take you from a place of not feeling so fulfilled to a serene and satisfying life. The daily part is what you can practice literally every day to move yourself to positive changes and, ultimately, happiness.

Remember Robin Hood and his Merry Men? Robin Hood was a highly skilled archer and swordsman, an outlaw hero. He fought for the rights of the oppressed against the evil sheriff of Nottingham. That sheriff was enforcing oppressive forest laws. In those days Sherwood was one of the royal forests, and the law protected the game inside the forest, so it was only the king who benefited. Meanwhile, ordinary people with meager livelihoods could not hunt there or use the land. Punishment was extreme—they would be blinded or have their hands cut off if caught. Certainly, that caused substantial anger and resentment. Robin Hood broke the forest laws and got away with it. He became the conquering hero who robbed from the rich and gave to the poor.

Robin Hood had followers and fellow outlaws called the Merry Men. Some famous followers were Little John and Friar Tuck. Maid Marian was Robin Hood's love interest. The sheriff of Nottingham was under a tremendous amount of pressure to capture Robin Hood. I will not tell you the end of the story.

What does this have to do with anything except it is interesting? Your life has probably been one where you have experienced oppression. That means unjust treatment, control, mental pressure, or distress. I think we all could fit in one of those categories. We have been down and out at some point and time, either emotionally, physically, mentally, financially, relationally, or spiritually. The evil sheriff reminds me of the evil Satan, who has done his best to see that we stay diminished and depleted. However, God bats last; even when the game is tied up, bases are loaded, and you have two outs, it's up to you to at least get the third base runner in. God will see you through the game of life. It's His character to do that. Instead of "you're out," we hear "safe." It's awesome, and with God it's always doable.

The Merry Men and Maid Marian are support. That support has major importance in helping a person get through the trials of life and truly add to the merriment of life. They are our Merry Men and Women. Merry Animals count as well.

As you read through the many concerns that are so common for us all, you will meet more than your Merry group of supporters. Some characters you can personally relate to, and others you know as family, friends, coworkers, or neighbors, such as Naomi Naysayer, Charlie Cheerless, Garrett Grumbly, Melancholy Marvin, Randy Regret, and Angry Angie. There is also the Fear Family and the Worry Family. No problem, though; there is also Warmhearted Wanda, Positive Penelope, and Leroy Learning to help you make some headway through the tough stuff life has thrown your way and my way. I made it through my depression, anxiety, worry, fear, disappointments, regrets, and a ton of stress. I have full confidence you can too. I trust you will be a success story as you utilize the coping skills and grow through self-understanding. Keep the skills near in your fanny pack, literally or figuratively.

Enjoy, and may God bless you on your journey to wholeness.

Anxiety

Anxiety, Fame, and a Situation

It would actually be a thrill to come in first place for something, whether it be for a bowling tournament, first place for a design, a race, or just about anything. There is also a first place in another category, and that is anxiety, as the first place or number one mental health concern in America. It is treatable, but oddly enough, only thirty-seven percent of the population seek treatment. I believe that is due to stigma. May it not be so! As you delve through the next seventeen chapters on mental health, glean into the numerous skills offered to put that to rest. Mental health is out in the open big time, and people are talking about it like they would discuss a good restaurant to go to.

Follow me and try to guess who is this famous person who decided to come out with her anxiety and panic diagnosis and her testimony to help herself and others. She grew up in childhood poverty with a very good mother and an absent alcoholic father. Her battle with anxiety didn't start until she went through a divorce. She gave an interview to Oprah, where she stated, "My anxiety attacks paralyzed me so completely, they made me confused, and I had no control over my body." She added that it felt like her body was on another planet. She struggled for a long time with disappointment in herself and for her son, as she chose to divorce and not keep the family intact. Her insight was quite apropos when she stated, "I want to be stable for myself, I don't expect someone else to give me stability." She stopped playing the large festivals due to her anxiety. The mystery person also had depression and, true to that disorder, was very withdrawn.

Any guesses as to who this famous female is? The first clue is she is from London. The second clue is she has sold over one hundred and twenty million records. The third clue is she has fifteen Grammys. Drum roll, the artist is Adele. In case you are wondering what this has to do with you—there are 275 million people globally who have an anxiety disorder, so that is a significant number of people who have a common denominator. That breaks down to about 170 million females and 106 million males (World Economic Forum). That staggering number means you are not alone by any means. Notice another thing we may have in common with her is the childhood struggles, the dysfunctional family, depression, financial hardships, and the disappointments. I am going to nickname her Awe-inspiring Adele because she took control of her life despite the disability.

In Matthew 14:22–32 there is an interesting Bible character named Peter that might have had anxiety or, at the very least, situational anxiety. That is anxiety that happens when in a new, unfamiliar, or uncomfortable situation. People are unsure and don't know what to expect, or it could be when in a certain situation they feel uncomfortable, as they had a negative experience with it. When the disciples were out in a boat, the wind notably picked up. Jesus came walking on the water toward them, but they were afraid, as they thought He was a ghost. Peter said, "Tell me to come to You on the water." The essence of the story is Peter started walking on the water when Jesus told him to come, but he became afraid and stated, "Lord, save me!" That was a very short but effective prayer. In spite of Peter seemingly taking his eyes off Jesus, the Lord came to him. See, the Lord comes to help us in our mess and distress. He comes to show us His presence. We just need to not take our eyes off the Lord. Certainly, that would decrease anxiety significantly.

There is a difference between anxiety, generalized anxiety disorder (GAD), and situational anxiety. Anxiety is a normal reaction to many different life events and includes a built-in warning system to threats or danger. The GAD involves a rather continuous stream of worrying with fear where you feel like you can't live a normal life, and situational anxiety happens when there is a specific situation. With situational anxiety you might have some dread or panic when you have to go on a job interview, meet potential in-laws for the first time, or give a speech. With GAD you can feel chronic anxiety without any particular trigger.

Skills to try:

1. If you are aware of an occasion coming up that could cause nervousness, then prepare ahead of time for it. Take care of your emotional needs. Also, for the upcoming occasion, wear something that you feel good in so your confidence increases. Do you have a routine that relaxes you? Humming and singing relaxes, and so does taking a shower or bath. Smell some lavender.

2. You will need to notice your body symptoms, such as you feel a nervous stomach or your breathing increases, and then start to soothe yourself.

3. Try to do something physical to divert the nervous energy to an activity.

4. Notice if you are having any negative thoughts, as they

will cause it to blow up bigger in your mind. Dispute the negative thinking. When your mind tells you something like you shouldn't go because someone there will judge you, then tell it no; that is not reality, and there is no reason for that erroneous thought. You expect to not miss out but will actually have a good time. Ask yourself, "Is the event really dangerous?"

5. Try to figure out what triggers your anxiety and, if possible, limit time with that activity. If it is work and you cannot do anything about that, then make sure you are not having too much caffeine and you are practicing deep breathing. Eat right and sleep enough.

6. When you have finished the event that has caused you GAD or situational anxiety and you see you got through it, then give yourself a good pat of congratulations for it and again do something relaxing as a reward.

7. Demonstrate courage.

8. Having a plan B will help ease anxiety, as you know that if it does not pan out as expected, you have an alternate route. Tell yourself like a car that has to change direction due to construction, you will easily just go with a different plan.

9. Call on a friend who is good at calming you down if needed for support before, during, and after the event.

Isaiah 35:4a (NIV), "Say to those with fearful hearts, 'Be strong, do not fear; your God will come.'"

These are words of comfort. There will always be times we have anxiety, but it says God will come to our aid. Looks like He Himself will come. How marvelous!

Response:

_____

_____

_____

_____

_____

_____

_____

_____

_____

_____

_____

_____

_____

_____

_____

_____

_____

_____

_____

_____

_____

_____

_____

_____

_____

How David Quieted His Soul

Anxiety can happen to anybody, and it is normal. What's not so normal is when the anxiety is about regular things, and it is intense and excessive, with a cousin of worry and fear attached at your hip. Sometimes a person cannot say what they are anxious about. It can be about losing control or about something bad that might happen. Anxiety can be gradual and range in severity from mild to a full-blown panic attack. Anxiety can include a rapid heartbeat, muscle tension, trembling, weakness, feeling impending doom, and not being able to concentrate due to worry.

Panic, on the other hand, is intense, sudden, and disruptive, with an attached intense fear even when there is no real danger or cause. It occurs spontaneously for no apparent reason. Panic can include physical reactions such as shortness of breath, heart palpitations, shakiness, feeling of choking, chest pain, or numbness. Medical conditions may need to be ruled out.

Why does anxiety happen? Research suggests a hereditary influence, chemical imbalance in the brain, long periods of stress, trauma, illnesses, sudden changes to the environment, sudden losses, or certain personality types. Research states people tend to develop anxiety in adolescence or in their twenties. One in three adolescents is affected. There are 40 million adults in the US (19.1 percent) that have an anxiety disorder, with the most common age group of those being thirty to forty-four years of age. A panic experience affects 6 million in the US (4.7 percent) of the population, with the same age group being the most common. Women are more affected than men.

There are several Bible characters who experienced anxiety or panic. David was one of them. He had to have panicked when he and his men returned to their camp, Ziklag, and found it destroyed by fire, and all the men's wives and children were taken captive (1 Samuel 30). It says he and his men wept until there were no more tears left. Great fear had to have been on them as well as feelings of helplessness and hopelessness. David's answer was to find strength in the Lord and inquire of the Lord what to do next. Anxiety may be eliminated or at least reduced if you can make good decisions that will prevent it or keep it from reaching intense levels. For instance, I have wondered if David left all those women and children without protection. We don't know. Could he have done something different so he would have had no regrets?

Skills to try:

1. Can some of what causes your anxiety be eliminated by improving your decision-making?

2. List ways you encourage yourself to get through the rough times.

3. David needed an immediate way to reduce his anxiety. The Word says he was "greatly distressed." Of course, that was a very intense circumstance. Since anxiety is focused on the future, take a moment and focus on the present. Ask yourself if anything needs to be done right away. If nothing, then come back to the situation when calmer. David's men were talking of stoning him, so he asked God whether to pursue the raiding party and whether he would overtake them. God answered him affirmatively. It pays tremendously and would be a perfect plan to inquire of the One who sees the whole picture. He is the ability in our inability.

First Samuel 30:6 (NIV), "David found strength in the Lord his God."

David had a personal relationship with the Lord. Those who

raided his camp and took all his family and possessions could not take that away from him. The Lord is the greatest resource of all resources.

Response:

_____

_____

_____

_____

_____

_____

_____

_____

_____

_____

_____

_____

_____

_____

_____

_____

_____

_____

_____

_____

You Are Definitely Not Alone

Some days you might feel like the rooster, and some days you feel like the spring chicken. You might even feel like the leghorn chicken. The rooster likes to wake up early to announce loudly, "Good morning. I am here, world; let's go forage for food." Is that too much noise and happy feelings too early in the day? For sure, okay, are you more like the spring chicken? That means "a young person" or a young chicken for eating. They are hardy but not friendly. They can really lay eggs. Wait. "Lay an egg" means you produced a flop or are unsuccessful. No, that's not good; you may have been feeling like that for far too long. I wish for you to be like the Orpington chicken. They have a quiet disposition, are docile, friendly, very gentle, calm, and rarely get cranky. They make great mothers and enjoy the company of humans. They are a healthy breed and thrive in most environments. That sounds like good mental health. And that's no foul!

The statistics for anxiety issues are almost staggering. It depends on which resource you use, but there are four to ten different anxiety disorders. I hope to normalize your anxiety symptoms by letting you know how common it is and that many others have the same concerns. I will give you the most common anxiety disorders. Anxiety is very treatable, but many do not seek treatment. Please consider an evaluation with a doctor if it appears to be altering your life.

1. *Generalized anxiety disorder:* Affects 6.8 million people in the US or 3.1 percent. It is persistent and excessive anxiety with worry about one's life, activities, and routines. The worry is out of proportion to the actual circumstance and is difficult to control.

2. *Panic disorder*: Affects 6 million people or 2.7 percent

of the US population. It is sudden feelings of intense anxiety with fear or terror that can reach a peak within minutes (panic attacks).

3. *Social anxiety disorder or social phobia:* Affects 15 million people in the US or 7 percent. It involves high levels of anxiety, fear, and avoidance of social situations.

4. *Separation anxiety disorder*: Affects 4 to 10 percent of US children and 0.9 to 1.9 percent of US adults. It is the fear of being away from home or loved ones.

5. *Specific phobias:* Affects 19 million or 9.1 percent of the US population. It is major anxiety when exposed to an object or situation one wishes to avoid. For example, snakes, heights, or flying.

6. *Agoraphobia*: Affects 1.8 million adults in the US or 2 percent of the US population. This type of anxiety disorder causes one to fear and avoid places or situations where one may feel trapped, helpless, or embarrassed.

7. *Anxiety disorder due to a medical condition*: Statistics unavailable. Symptoms of intense anxiety or panic directly caused by a physical condition.

One of the most effective ways to get anxiety under control quickly is to breathe deep. Deep breathing is also called diaphragmatic breathing, abdominal breathing, and belly breathing. This will help you move from your stressor to a calm rhythm. It is good for your nervous system.

Skill to try:

1. Find a quiet, comfortable place to sit or lie down. Take a slow, regular breath in through your nose. Breathe in to a count of four. Allow your chest and lower belly to rise to fill your lungs. Hold for four seconds. Slowly exhale through your mouth for four seconds. Now try the same but taking a deep breath. Repeat until you feel calm.

Psalm 94:19 (NIV), "When anxiety was great within me, your consolation brought joy to my soul."

The Lord has a special kind of comfort like none other. It is called His presence. He will give you renewed hope and gladness.

Response:

_____

_____

_____

_____

_____

_____

_____

_____

_____

_____

_____

_____

_____

_____

_____

_____

The Sky Is Falling

A sweet little chicken named Chicken Little thought the sky was falling. The story is from a children's tale with the same name. An acorn fell on her head, which made her think that the sky was falling. She ended up telling five other animals of her "belief." She believed she just needed to tell the king about this problem. It ends up that a slick fox was trying to lure all those animals away from the king so he could eat them. However, the animals reached the king, who cleared up the wrong thinking.

There could be more than one moral of the story. What is your interpretation? Could she have had a mistaken belief, paranoia, worry, fear or anxiety, or some of the above? The sly fox is like Satan, who wants to steal, kill, and destroy. There is quite the contrast, as Satan comes to destroy and the Lord comes to give life.

A mistaken belief is a misconception resulting from incorrect information. They are lies and misbeliefs that people adopt about the world, and they can hold a person back from fully enjoying life. Everybody has uncertainties, and those doubts and beliefs sound reasonable. To us they are the truth, but they are not reality. Misbeliefs are a case of a stress reaction. With stress and anxiety, the body reacts, and one ends up perceiving the events of life as overwhelming. There are many things that catch one off guard or pile up because yesterday's stressors are still hanging around. It is like wearing yesterday's dirty gym socks that stink. Get rid of them. It is not so easy to just get rid of one's stress, but the principle is to discard it or at the least manage through it.

The sweet little chicken could have had some paranoia. Paranoia is a symptom of some mental health problems but not a diagnosis itself. It is not the kind that is delusional per se, but the kind that is distrustful or suspicious and senses danger everywhere. If you experience anxiety, depression, or low self-esteem, there is a probability you will have some paranoid thoughts. You will feel on the edge and worry more than usual and interpret things in a negative way. Paranoia can be considered a self-centered fear. People with paranoia usually view themselves as inadequate and unworthy. They feel like people in general will reject them. They believe that their every word and action about their paranoid fears is correct, but that is inaccurate.

Paranoia is thought to be caused by genes, brain chemistry, stressful or traumatic life events, or a combination. Insomnia plays a big role as well, as hallucinations may occur. Paranoia can be a symptom of some physical illnesses, such as Parkinson's disease and Alzheimer's disease. Some medications can cause paranoia. If a person feels isolated, it can trigger paranoid feelings. Some recreational drugs can trigger paranoia. Paranoia can cause anxiety, and anxiety can cause paranoia. Chicken Little thought there would be a catastrophe.

King Saul had a serious case of paranoia. David had become very popular and had much success with his leadership role over the armies. The king became angry and suspicious of him. He saw David as a threat to his kingdom. He became jealous, which turned to paranoia and then to thoughts of murdering David when there was no cause to do so. The sad result to the state of mind of the king was he acted like he had a serious depression along with that paranoia. He lost the Spirit of God and Satan entered the king as if he had whistled and invited him in (1 Samuel 18:22).

On the positive side, Chicken Little seemed to be a problem solver. It is okay to be afraid at times. We all are. She sought an answer from the highest authority, the king. So should we. We get that from our highest authority—Christ. I think she knew she was little, but she took charge, so size did not matter, but determination did. We can feel small against a big world and a big problem. That is intimidating in itself. She picked up friends on her way to the king, which tells us she liked and valued support. Again, isn't that a smart move?

Now about that slick fox. Foxes like to eat chickens; just ask a farmer. The fox is manipulative, sneaky, and an opportunist. He is just like the devil, who sees a chance to exploit someone who has fear. The fivesome were "lured" to an isolated den. The animals were able to come to their senses and realize the trap before it was too late. Satan can and will attack us whenever he can, but when people are physically or emotionally vulnerable, at a weak point he might find it easier to deceive.

Be careful what you say to yourself. If you start the day thinking it will not go well, then anxiety is self-created. It is anticipating the worst before it even happens. It is anxious self-talk. The power of your words will take you down or bring you up. You don't want to think the sky is falling (life is going badly, and the outlook is bleak). You want your inner voice to inform you that "all is well" or "you can do this."

Skills to try:

1. Recognize when you are having paranoia, feeling worried, fearful, or anxious. Stop the thoughts right away. Picture a red stop sign. Replace the anxious thought with supportive and calming statements to yourself. An example is to tell yourself that you are all right and you can deal with the situation.
2. Consider trying cognitive behavioral therapy (CBT).

This therapy will look at how your thoughts affect your behavior and how to replace the inaccurate thoughts with more realistic ones.

3. Drug and alcohol use and lack of sleep can prompt paranoia, so make any necessary lifestyle changes.

4. Relaxation exercises can reduce worry and stress, which will exacerbate paranoia.

5. As hard as this is, you need to switch from self-doubt to self-belief. Try and understand where that mistaken belief came from. Acknowledge your emotions and thoughts, and take care of yourself.

6. Take a serious look at your part, your actions, and how that influences your thoughts and emotions.

First Peter 5:7 (NIV), "Cast all your anxiety on Him because He cares for you."

I hope you caught the word "all." "To cast" means "to throw upon." Christ desires very much to carry our cares. Just think that if we become increasingly dependent on the Lord, how much stress will decrease? It is a good trade.

Response:

_____

_____

_____

_____

_____

_____

_____

_____

_____

_____

_____

_____

_____

_____

_____

_____

_____

_____

_____

_____

_____

Anxiety and the Wickie

I expect most people will not know what a wickie is. I had to look it up and, in so doing, realized there is a great comparison to having anxiety. A wickie is the nickname for a lighthouse keeper. The name is derived from the task of trimming the wick of the lamps. There are seven hundred lighthouses in the United States with Michigan having the most. In the world there are more than 21,600 lighthouses. The United States National Park Service states there are two hundred active lighthouses maintained by the Navigational Aid Center, whereas only thirty-three are now staffed.

The early years of the wickies had much to manage. They had to deal with isolation, endure violent storms, and be ready to respond to the occasional shipwreck. One such wickie said in the storm of 1950 at Pond Island Lighthouse, Maine, he sometimes slept in a life jacket in case he had to do a rescue or go out and ring a bell if it was foggy weather.

Until the invention of the light bulb, the light for the lighthouse came from a flame. This meant there were risks of fire and lead. There were the actual perils involved in rescuing if a boat or ship capsized. The weather could be perilous and unpredictable. Before electricity and automation in the 1960s, it was up to the wickie to ensure the massive lens kept spinning all day. The lens could weigh up to two and a half tons. The lens was floated in liquid mercury, which the lighthouse aids breathed and touched daily, causing mercury poisoning. The extreme isolation from those early days caused a host of issues mentally.

So now you may be wondering where I am going with this information. For creative giggles pretend you are the wickie and you have anxiety. Storms, the possible fires and mercury poisoning, and the harsh loneliness cause it to be worse. You don't know when these events will occur, and your anxiety is about the future. So you stay on edge daily. You know you need to maintain your equipment, as it requires cleaning, repairing, painting, and keeping the light maintained and burning at night, but you go about your day feeling nervous. With every "what-if" your vigilance makes things worse. You regularly feel "on guard" and worried. You circle your lighthouse looking for the threat of a storm even though it is just a lovely breeze. That is you magnifying things. Although you are doing your job, you take it too far and cause yourself to be strained and jumpy with every sudden noise. You lose your focus and feel suspicious of people, as some of your overreacting has made you irritable and somewhat hostile, which is unlike you. You find it hard to talk to others, but that is okay with you, as all you have is birds and chickens around you.

People with anxiety issues often believe that isolating themselves will reduce their anxiety. This is fear-based and inaccurate. However, social support is powerful. It is understood that having anxiety makes it hard to meet others and attend social events. The anxious person thinks negatively and seems to take on thinking that going out and socializing is either "safe" or "dangerous," so they play it safe and don't go.

Vigilance is necessary for things we need to be alert to, but hypervigilance is being fearful, anxious, and on edge. Being so hypervigilant can affect your existing relationships. If you are in a regular state of alertness, then you will come across as being needy and clingy. If you have to check your surroundings so much, then you most likely have trust issues. The vigilant person may find themselves too emotional and easily cry and act out in other ways.

So let's get you doing what you enjoy in your daily life without the vigilance and anxiety.

Skills to try:

1. Take a break as often as is plausible. This includes the simple exercise of stretching, breathing exercises, muscle relaxation, or meditation/prayer. Whatever helps you move will help your mental and physical health. It's all about relaxing!

2. Talk to people. Don't isolate. It can lead to increasing your anxiety, and depression may also set in as well, as cortisol levels increase; thus, it can cause health issues.

3. Don't overthink. Distractions help with that.

4. Have personal care—things you do to help you relax, such as taking a bubble bath, eating your favorite food, taking time to read, time on the hammock or bench, fishing, or taking a walk. It is about doing the things that bring you a sense of calm. Make a list and begin to incorporate them.

5. If things are overwhelming, then it is a good idea to get a mental health professional to help you not just be aware of your surroundings but enjoy them, as well as give you skills to reduce anxiety and eliminate your fears.

Psalm 23:1–3a (NKJV), "The Lord is my shepherd; I shall not want. He makes me to lie down in green pastures; He leads me beside the still waters. He restores my soul."

"My" indicates a personal relationship. David is looking at God as the One who provides for his needs. God Himself wants to rest us. We all need rest, and we need to rest in Him. In Hebrew "still waters" means "restful waters or refreshment." "To restore" means "to give back, return, recover, repair, or renew." We all need our soul restored, and God knows how to do that.

Response:

_____

_____

_____

_____

_____

_____

_____

_____

_____

_____

_____

_____

_____

_____

_____

_____

_____

_____

_____

_____

_____

_____

Maybe You Are Keeping Anxiety Going, Part One

Before we talk about you, see if you can tell what animal is quite anxious. These animals' movements are frantic and haphazard. If you scare them, they will freeze, bear their teeth, and hiss at you. They can get hit by cars, mangled by dogs and other critters, as well as get fleas and a parasitic worm. And then there are the humans who sadly hurt them on purpose. They are slow, so they do not do well catching food; therefore, they are relegated to eating slow things like snails and grubs. They are noted as being dazed and frantic. What is your guess? You would know right away if I said they play dead. It's the opossum. That playing-dead thing is faking cardiac arrest when they feel desperate ("The Opossum: L.A.'s Most Anxious Animal," by Tim Loc, August 15, 2016).

Poor opossum. However, people are not too far from this anxious behavior. We can get worked up and have panic attacks. We have all been haphazard and anxious at points in our lives. Haphazard meaning lack of direction. Been there and done that. Our playing dead is like our body going into the freeze response when we are afraid. That means the person is very alert but unable to move.

There are maintaining causes that tend to keep anxiety going. Let's examine several. They are paraphrased from *The Anxiety and Phobia Workbook*, third edition, by Edmund J. Bourne, PhD. Scripture and explanations are from this author.

Do you avoid phobic situations? As long as you continue to avoid dealing with a phobic situation, activity, or object, the phobia will remain in place. Overcoming a phobia means you unlearn certain responses while relearning others. You can learn to tolerate and be comfortable in any phobic situation if you approach it in sufficiently small steps.

Are you running an internal monologue—your self-talk—that anticipates the worst before it happens? The anxiety is created by statements you make to yourself, such as "What if this or that?" It is simply worry. Do you use scare talk, which can lead to a full-blown panic attack? Learn to recognize anxiety-provoking self-talk, stop it, and replace it with more supportive and calming statements.

Your negative self-talk comes from underlying mistaken beliefs about yourself, others, and "the way the world is." Recognizing your own particular mistaken beliefs is the first step toward letting them go. We take these beliefs for granted and assume they reflect reality. An example is "I am unimportant." A positive affirmation is needed to counter that, such as "I am valuable."

Denying feelings can contribute to a state of free-floating anxiety. This is when you feel vaguely anxious and don't know why. Expressing your feelings can result in a reduced level of anxiety. Know what you are feeling and allow your feelings some form of expression.

If you are prone to anxiety and phobias, you will tend to act submissively. You need to develop an assertive style of communicating that allows you to express yourself in a direct, forthright manner. You may be afraid of imposing on others, or you may not want to compromise your self-image as someone who is pleasant. You are afraid that you will alienate the one person you are dependent on for security. Some ways to be assertive are to look directly at another person when addressing them, maintain an open posture, and stay calm. You can also become aware of your own feelings, wants, and needs. Say "no" to requests you do not want to meet.

Skills to try:

1. They are listed in the above paragraphs. Practice what pertains to you.

Proverbs 3:5–6 (NIV), "Trust in the Lord with all your heart and lean not on your own understanding; in all your ways acknowledge Him, and He will make your path straight."

If you lean on your own understanding, then it seems like you took charge and left the Lord out. Trusting the Lord means you believe in Him and depend on Him and you will allow Him to show you the way.

Response:

_____

_____

_____

_____

_____

_____

_____

_____

_____

_____

_____

_____

_____

_____

_____

_____

_____

_____

_____

_____

Maybe You Are Keeping Anxiety Going, Part Two

The previous pages were about causes that might be keeping your anxiety going. They are from the book *The Anxiety and Phobia Workbook*, third edition, written by Edmund J. Bourne, PhD. All are paraphrased. Scripture and explanation are from this author.

Common to the background of many people with anxiety disorders is a sense of insecurity. This insecurity comes from a variety of conditions in childhood, including parental neglect, abuse, abandonment, overprotection, over-criticism, betrayal, as well as alcohol or chemical dependence in the family. These individuals are unaware of how to love and nurture themselves. The lack of these skills serves to perpetuate anxiety. One will need to learn skills to be good to themself. This is about developing the ability to give yourself what you did not get growing up. However, insecurity can come from not accepting certain situations, people, or themself and fearing failure. They make assumptions that people in their sphere are out to get them. This has to do with a person's past or personal fears.

Muscle tension can be a problem, as it tends to restrict your breathing, and with restricted breathing, you may experience anxiety. If your body is tense, your mind has a tendency to race. Tense muscles help keep your feelings suppressed, which can increase anxiety. The solution is to incorporate relaxation and exercise into your lifestyle.

Stimulants such as caffeine and nicotine can aggravate anxiety and leave you more vulnerable to panic attacks. Sugar and food additives can aggravate or even cause panic attacks. There is a connection between how you feel and what you eat.

A high-stress lifestyle will perpetuate anxiety. If one learns to manage their stress from all items from the previous page, this page, and other factors, such as time management, type A personalities, and communication, it will go a long way in reducing stress. Also, it is helpful to lower your expectations not because you will do less of a job but because you may be having perfectionism tendencies, thus worrying about how others perceive you. Find a balance between work and life. You are not failing if you adjust expectations or goals, so don't shut down!

People who feel like their life has meaning, purpose, and a sense of direction experience relief from anxiety and phobias. Without purpose you may have boredom and feelings of confinement, as you are not realizing your potential. There is much healing and benefit to be obtained by developing your spiritual life.

Skills to try:

1. The above paragraphs are food for thought. It is up to you to delve further into the area you feel pertains to you, research it more fully, and use the skills.

2. You will keep feeling insecure and anxious if you keep comparing yourself to others. Of course, make improvements if possible, but it's your life you are carving out, not somebody else's. Trying to be better than others seems to never end and will cause you to be unduly disappointed.

Matthew 11:28 (NIV), "Come to me all you who are weary and burdened, and I will give you rest."

Jesus promises us rest, and that sounds mighty good with the load and weight we tend to carry. We are to leave it at the cross or feet of the Lord. He Himself will give us rest.

Response:

_____

_____

_____

_____

_____

_____

_____

_____

_____

_____

_____

_____

_____

_____

_____

_____

_____

_____

_____

Phobias

Here is a cute little joke for you—I have a phobia of German sausage. Yes, I fear the wurst.

That was to make you smile. However, phobias are no laughing matter. Read on.

Phobias are an irrational, intense fear or aversion to something, a situation, or an activity. Phobias are recorded as affecting 19 million people in the United States. Phobias are classified as generalized anxiety disorders. The difference between fear and phobias is the extent to which anxiety is involved. Phobias cause extreme dread and are out of proportion to the object or situation. Some phobias can start in early childhood, but an onset age is normally fifteen to twenty. Women are slightly more likely to have a phobia than men.

Children have phobias about the dark, monsters, animals, insects, heights, going to the doctor/dentist, germs, not being near their loved ones/abandonment, and change in schools or being late for school. Teenagers have phobias about spiders, enclosed spaces, heights, germs, becoming ill, death, parents divorcing, and not doing well in school/passing their grade. I even hear there is a new phobia of fear of not having their cell phone. It is called nomophobia.

For adults the fear of public speaking, called glossophobia, affects 75 percent of the population, so that's very familiar to many of us. Other common phobias are fear of snakes, spiders, heights, germs, dogs, and flying. Parents have phobias about stranger danger, bullying, accidents, illness, and injury to their children.

For adults the reaction to phobias is usually a feeling of powerlessness to control their phobia. They have intense anxiety and panic. The distress is heavy. Avoidance is the go-to coping skill. Their phobia can cause strained relationships, trouble traveling, and work issues. Teenagers feel confused and even disoriented, as well as have anxiety and panic. For example, if the teenager has a required class of speech and they have a fear of speaking in public, they will likely panic. They feel that others don't understand. Children will cry, throw tantrums, freeze, and become clingy.

Skills to try:

1. Get started. Be willing to face your fear/phobia. Encourage talk about what the phobia is (if dealing with children/teens) and that you will take it seriously. Validate their feelings.

2. Have some support and take someone with you if you choose to face it. Apply no pressure on yourself.

3. Practice or try desensitizing yourself to your fear/phobia. For example, if it is public speaking, practice with one person, then practice some more and in a more public place. If it is getting on an elevator, then go to the building that has an elevator one day, and the next time go closer etcetera.

4. Try relaxation techniques, such as muscle relaxation, breathing, visualization, using reassuring self-talk, and meditation/prayer. Art therapy is especially helpful for children. Music is favorable for teenagers. Have patience with yourself and your children. Change takes time.

5. Recognize that you are having a panic attack, so it will be temporary. Tell yourself you will be okay. If it is a medical emergency, seek immediate medical help.

6. If it is a trigger that overwhelms you, try closing your eyes to reduce the stimuli.

7.   Seek professional help if life is becoming out of control.

Psalm 34:17 (NIV), "The righteous cry out, and the Lord hears them: He delivers him from them all."

It is a terrible emotion to feel alone, distressed, and even panicked when we are in need. But for the righteous, the Lord hears us and delivers us. That includes delivering us from Satan's traps.

Response:

_____

_____

_____

_____

_____

_____

_____

_____

_____

_____

_____

_____

_____

_____

Get Calm

Here is a riddle for you. What weighs about a thousand pounds or more but is not overweight? In fact, it does not usually have enough to eat. It is also on the endangered list. Any guess? It's the manatee. I have included this fabulous mammal because it is kind, peaceful, and docile. They are friendly to people. Do you want to be calm and have a soothing disposition? How do you think it would feel to be less confrontational in general and have people enjoy being around you, as you do not seem to have strong emotions that rise up and spoil the moments in the friendships? And how about being without that edginess and unrest so your blood pressure is normal? Read on.

C—stands for comfort. If we feel comfortable, whether at home, work, or other places, we will have less worry and stress. Especially if we feel comfortable at home, then we also feel like we have some control. It is within our ability to set our home up to achieve just that. Have you decluttered? Have you painted the walls with the colors you find relaxing? Have you acquired comfortable furniture and added a cushion, quilt, or soothing plants? Do you have nick knacks or pictures on display that make you smile? Everything about your home or workplace should be peaceful. It should feel like your sanctuary. When your environment is not tranquil, you feel anxiety, fear, or stress.

There is a time when being comfortable may not be good. That is when you stay in your comfort zone and, therefore, do not try to achieve your goals. It may cause you to settle, be stagnant, and not grow. Only you can decide. Find the right balance.

A—stands for affirmations. They are statements you say to

45

yourself that are positive and make you feel better. They motivate and create self-empowerment. For example, if you tell yourself you are worthy, loved, can do the job, and finish school, etcetera, it creates a feeling that you are capable of doing that. It is good to give yourself a positive affirmation on a daily basis.

L—stands for laugh. Laughter is a great medicine. It is good for the spirit, soul, and body. It will chase away your lousy feeling, and at least for the time, you can destress and forget why you were upset. It relaxes the body and stimulates endorphins, so you feel better. It will create connectedness, as you make others smile and laugh. Healthy laughter will cause others to want to be around you.

Here is a joke for you—A man asked his wife what she wanted for her birthday. She replied, "I'd love to be ten again." So on her birthday he whisked her off to a theme park where they went on all the rides. After those five hours at the park, her head was reeling, and her stomach queasy. She made it home and collapsed into bed. He then asked her, "Was it like being ten again?" With one eye open, she moaned, "I meant a size ten dress."

Okay, you know you liked it, right?

M—Stands for meditation. It helps one remain calm and reduce stress but does not involve communion with God. However, for today's skill I will substitute that for prayerful reflection. Prayer is about deliberate communication with the Lord, where you can learn of Him, grow closer to Him, and find wisdom, guidance, strength, peace, hope, forgiveness, and power. We can come into the Lord's presence with thanksgiving, praise, and worship and ask for what we need or intercede for others.

Billy Graham stated, "True prayer is a way of life, not just for use in cases of emergency. Make it a habit, and when the need arises you will be in practice."

Skills to try:

1. The four are listed above in the acronym *CALM*—find comfort, make affirmations, laugh, and meditate/pray. If there is something in those examples in which you don't see yourself, then spend some time making the changes that will add to your life's fullness.

2. Find some funny/corny jokes and tell them to someone. You will enjoy just looking them up.

3. The mind controls the body, so it is imperative to not spend so much time "in your head." Focus on your body by deliberately breathing and walking in nature. Be aware that whatever you focus on grows within you, and thus, you may become that. If you focus on the things that make you nervous, that grows within you, and you become a nervous person. Focus on the fruits of the spirit as mentioned in Galatians 5:22, which are love, joy, peace, patience, kindness, goodness, faithfulness, gentleness, and self-control, and the principle applies that it grows within you, and you become that. How about focusing on being imitators of God as it says in Ephesians 5:1, and what grows in us is Christlikeness?

Joshua 1:8 (NIV), "Do not let this book of the Law depart from your mouth; meditate on it day and night, so that you may be careful to do everything written in it. Then you will be prosperous and successful."

To meditate in this passage is to think deeply and prepare your mind and heart. The bonus is we prosper and become successful. Sounds like a very good thing to do.

Response:

_____

_____

_____

_____

_____

_____

_____

_____

_____

_____

_____

_____

_____

_____

_____

_____

_____

_____

_____

_____

Depression

I Am Your Storm

"I am your storm" is depression talking. Hold on! You have an anchor and a tugboat as well. You are the ship; your helpers are the tugboat and crew, and the anchor is your hope. Let's read deeper into this.

If a storm rages at sea and there is a threat that the ship can sink, the captain can deploy a "sea anchor." It looks like a parachute, is connected to the bow, and keeps the ship aerodynamically pointed into the wind. No matter what direction the wind blows, a sea anchor keeps the vessel afloat until the storm subsides. Remember that wind is your storm, and the negative talk and depressive feelings are as well. However, we are anchored to the Lord, our living hope.

Every ship has some sort of steering system. Of course, for this analogy, that is the Lord giving us direction. Satan, for all intents and purposes, will be the propulsion power as it pushes and pulls to try to drive us in the wrong direction. The potential is that it can suck a person under. No way, don't let that happen! You are not going to sink because you have that anchor. It will keep you from capsizing. The anchor is our symbol of hope.

The tugboat's job is to guide the ship through constricted areas. Those vessels might be a barge or a ship that has broken down and needs repair. Depression makes us feel broken down and in need of repair. The barge does not move independently; they are towed or tugged by other vessels. They are designed to be very strong. The tugboat will likely have a captain, mate, deckhand, oiler, and engineer, to name a few. Our friends and family represent the tugboat and its crew; they add strength and the push we need sometimes to get to our harbor (our shelter). They help us when in a depressed state, or I should say if they are allowed to be helpers when a person is down and out.

Seagoing tugboats are designed to operate at sea for long periods. They are strong and powerful. The crew is in it for the twenty-four-hours-and-seven-days-a-week responsibility, and that can last for weeks or months. Sleep can be interrupted; weather could be hazardous with ice and snow, and working on wet surfaces can be risky. There seems to be considerable noise all the time. But the crew (our loved ones) want to be there.

Let's compare that to working with a depressed person, which can be beneficial, as you are helping someone you care about. You hopefully will see progress as your friend or family member comes back to life as their "storm of depressed life" dissipates. You can be part of the follow-up.

Skills to try:

1. If you are depressed, start by choosing activities that you will actually complete to get you back to moving again. Suggestions are strength training, swimming, gardening, hiking, antique shopping, getting in a sauna,

going to a library, and art, for example.

2. Include a friend to help you keep momentum and add to making the activity more enjoyable. People that care about you and are positive bring a good vibe. Have a stimulating conversation or a heart-to-heart one, whatever is needed. Include some laughter.

3. It may have been a long time since you decided you wanted to be "tugged or moved." So start small with your plan and take breaks as needed.

4. Write down three things that were positive about your day. Tell yourself why it was good and how you can add more of that goodness into your day. Do the same for tomorrow for a week, then examine how you feel.

5. Spend time in another environment. The analogy here is the sea, but it could be the beach, a mall, the mountains, a park, the woods, or another neighborhood or town.

6. Notice what you focus on. Keep your thoughts about positive things and items and people you appreciate. Chart what time of day and which day it is a good focus or not so good so you can adjust for the people, places, and things that may be around at that time. For instance, if you noticed your mood dropped lower when the couple Henry and Hallie Happy came around, it may mean you are missing that joy that is potentially in a relationship for yourself.

Second Corinthians 12:9 (NIV), "He said to me 'My grace is sufficient for you, for my power is made perfect in weakness.' Therefore, I will boast all the more gladly about my weaknesses so that Christ's power may rest on me."

The apostle Paul believes that even if God does not answer his prayer and remove the thorn in his flesh or his weakness, God will give him grace to weather it. Any weakness he has will glorify God, as the power of Christ will rest on him.

Response:

_____

_____

_____

_____

_____

_____

_____

_____

_____

_____

_____

_____

_____

_____

_____

_____

_____

_____

Depression Wears Many Faces

Depression affects 21 million people in the United States. That is majorly common. It is a feeling that causes persistent sadness and loss of interest, and it affects how you think, feel, and behave. Depression can be a major depressive disorder (most common), situational depression (some event or stress in one's life), manic-depressive illness (bipolar disorder), or it could be chronic, as in dysthymia or cyclothymia. I have been there; I get it. You are getting my best skills in this book. I don't want you to just manage depression but overcome it as I did.

People sometimes pretend they are fine when the opposite is true. Depression on a face can look sad, apathetic, bored, guilty, irritated, tired, or angry, to name a few. They may also have some verbal expressions such as "Sometimes, I wonder if it is all worth it" or "I am stuck." Some behaviors are crying easily, neglecting routine and hygiene, loss of interest in people and activities, staying in bed for extended periods of time, and having many complaints. With seniors in particular, depression can manifest as headaches, fatigue, stomach issues, and joint pain.

People with depression have difficulty with their sense of fairness versus unfairness. They tend to look around and make comparisons. This is totally not helpful, as there will always be someone who seems to have it all. Maybe they do, and maybe they don't have it all. We do not see what goes on behind closed doors, and we don't see what God is doing in their life. An individual may have gone through a layoff, but another keeps their job. One person has been betrayed, and another has never had that experience. Somebody has had many losses, while another has never experienced any. Some people have multiple medical concerns, and another has perfect health. Do not look around for equality.

There was a prophet in the Bible (1 Kings 17) named Elijah who also wore the many faces of depression and made some depressive statements. God gave him the assignment to show the nation of Israel that Jehovah is the One true God, not Baal. Off he goes to confront the wicked King Ahab and defame his idol, Baal. A showdown was planned at Mount Carmel, where Elijah had stated to the people who gathered, "If the Lord is God, follow Him, but if Baal, follow him." Two bulls were put on two separate altars with no fire for the offering. Elijah would call on the Lord for the fire for his bull, and the priests would call on Baal for fire for theirs. Elijah seemed to enjoy insulting the priests of Baal as their god did not respond by bringing fire. Then Elijah prayed, and fire fell from heaven and burned up his offering. The result was the people returned to the Lord.

When Queen Jezebel heard this, she made a threat to kill Elijah. Elijah lost his courage even after that mighty display of power, so he ran far away and hid. Now we can identify fear, stress, great fatigue, self-pity, and being vulnerable with the unknown. It does sound like he struggled with the emotions we go through as well. I will not think any less of him because he had to have been physically and mentally depleted, let down, despondent, anxious, worried, and even terrified. That's human. For a man who was considered rough, tough, and very bold, we can sum up that he was overwrought. All that he did to defy the prophets of Baal—he stood alone and obeyed the Lord. That in itself is amazing.

Out of Elijah's mouth was a despairing statement, "I have had enough, Lord...take my life" (1 Kings 19:4, NIV). But God did not leave Elijah in that emotional turmoil. As he was contemplating his desire to die, he fell asleep, and an angel came and gave him food. An angel came a second time with food as well to nourish him for the next forty days of travel. The Lord instructed Elijah to stand on a mountain of God, as He was about to pass by. There came a powerful wind, an earthquake, and fire, but the Lord was not in those entities; then, there was a gentle whisper. Elijah heard the whisper. We must listen to the still, small voice of the Lord always, but how much more when "on edge" emotionally? God was showing Elijah His mercy, power, provision, and love.

Even those of us who are God-fearing people can have "It is enough, Lord" moments, but we must never let ourselves sink so deep in that despair. It essentially means we were focused on ourselves, took our eyes off the Lord, and forgot He is the God of miracles, sustaining care, and can strengthen us for the "defeat Baal" trials of life.

Skills to try:

1. Rather than deal with the possibility that self-pity has entered in as it is too hard to examine, some prefer sympathy, medication, or addiction substitutes. Is that you? In history I had self-pity. It happens; it's okay to feel that rotten for now, but do not stay there. Self-pity destroys motivation, so hopelessness enters your thinking. Excuses get made, and statements are frequent, such as "If you had my life, you'd feel the same way." Break free from such thinking.

2. Self-care is paramount. When a person is overtired, depression appears more easily.

3. Elijah had a servant that he dismissed. He was alone. Loneliness will wear you down. Identify a support system so they can monitor the ups and downs and help you regain your footing as well as make you accountable.

4. Read my pages on resiliency. Incorporate those skills to build a different mindset.

5. The body was not made to be inactive. Move if you are physically able to. If restricted, then try chair exercises. It may be hard to do, as you have to muster up energy, but the benefits will come from it.

6. Get in nature. Walk amongst the trees and grass, and smell the flowers. Look at the water or, better yet, get in it.

7. Take magnesium. Not having enough of this mineral can cause depression, anxiety, and fatigue.

Psalm 9:9 (NIV), "The Lord is a refuge for the oppressed, a stronghold in times of trouble."

David is writing this. "Oppressed" implies people were being abused by those who had control over them. "Refuge" means "shelter or protection from danger or trouble" (dictionary.com).

Response:

_____

_____

_____

_____

_____

_____

_____

_____

_____

_____

_____

_____

_____

_____

_____

_____

_____

_____

Get to the Roots

With depression there is always a cause or causes. I liken that to a tree with a root system. One can obviously see the tree but down below are the tap root, secondary roots, tertiary roots, and rootlets. We can see a person, but we do not see what is going on "underground emotionally." Sometimes what is going on with the tree can be obvious as it is in need of nutrients or water or is diseased. This is the same for the depressed person; it may show on the face or physically.

Possible causes of depression:

1. *Abuse*—if a person has been abused physically, emotionally, mentally, or sexually, it causes feelings of worthlessness and low self-esteem. It may even feel like a dagger to the heart. Recognize the signs of abuse and don't make excuses for the abuser. It is never okay. Seek support from family and friends and get professional help.

2. *Disappointment*—to live is to experience disappointment. Life happens, and people and events can disappoint. Check your expectations. Don't expect other people to make you happy. It will cause you to feel angry at anyone or everyone, including yourself. Have goals so you have something to look forward to.

3. *Medications*—certain drugs can increase your risk of depression. Please ask a doctor.

4. *Self-esteem problems*—do you have trouble with self-approval? Are your expectations unrealistic? Examine where this comes from. Stop listening to your inner critic.

5. *Conflicts with others*—unresolved conflicts create tension, stress, anxiety, and depression. It stores up frustra-

tion. Communicate and listen. There are two sides to the coin. Look for a win-win.

6. *Unfair comparisons*—you feel like you are lacking in an area where you made comparisons to someone having more than you. This will only cause you to feel less than and not good enough, as well as add pressure upon yourself. For example, if you are comparing yourself to someone younger, then stop that, as you cannot become younger. I can compare myself to someone tall, but it is futile, as I am short and won't ever be tall. Just work on yourself in an area you desire. Love and accept yourself.

7. *Death or loss*—it is normal to feel sadness or grief after a death or loss, but it can lead to depression if you are eventually unable to move on. Move on one day at a time and one step at a time. Support groups for grief are valuable.

8. *Ambivalence*—the sense of being trapped in an intolerable situation. Example: feeling trapped in a loveless marriage or feeling worthless. This will cause you to be always second-guessing and add anxiety to the already stressful situation. Take careful consideration of your options and take action.

9. *Illness*—your tolerance level is lowered during sickness. Stress causes people to have a harder time dealing with pain.

10. *Major events*—moving, divorcing, graduating, retiring, job loss, marriage, births, kids going off to college, deaths, and friends leaving can foster depression due to an imbalance in one's neurotransmitters. Many coping skills are included in this book for these situations.

11. *Rejection*—when the need to be loved does not get met, then depression can quickly happen. It is about pushing someone or something away. Rejection can come from a job loss, family, or betrayal. Do not fixate on injustice.

12. *Aging*—loss of control, loss of friends, medical issues, and financial concerns can lead to depression. See the

section on aging and depression for suggestions.

13. *Family background*—families carry the capacity to nurture or injure. Depression can happen due to criticism, lack of love, indifference, exposure to stressful situations throughout your life, and a genetic link. If you have an immediate relative, like a parent, with depression, then you have a two to three times greater risk of developing the condition. Know that a genetic predisposition does not mean you will get the disorder. Hereditary concerns are complex. If needed, seek treatment.

14. *Loneliness or lack of intimacy*—isolation is destructive to our well-being. God designed us to need each other. One must move past the loneliness to activities and people. See the chapters on loneliness.

15. Verywellmind.com reports there are *non-genetic causes of depression*. Those are brain chemistry (lower levels of neurotransmitters), changes in brain structure (brain may be physically and structurally different), hormones (thyroid, menopause, and pregnancy), and extreme stress.

16. *Lack of intimacy with God*—deep in each person is a vacuum that can only be filled by a personal relationship with the Lord. You are body, soul, and spirit. Consider developing your spiritual nature.

Skill to try:

1. 1. Look over the above list carefully. Where is adjustment needed? Be patient with yourself as you make adjustments one at a time and one day at a time. Chart your progress so you can see your improvements.

Matthew 3:10 (NIV), "The ax is already at the root of the trees, and every tree that does not produce good fruit will be cut down and thrown into the fire."

The scripture refers to judgment, but for coping skills, consider this: if you see yourself with any of these "roots of depression," cut them off if able to do or seek a mental health professional.

Response:

_____

_____

_____

_____

_____

_____

_____

_____

_____

_____

_____

_____

_____

_____

_____

_____

Maybe You Are Making Depression Worse

You are likely aware that you are depressed, but are there things you are doing that could be making it worse? You may feel like a fold-away bed. You know, the kind of hideaway bed that folds into a wall or closet. I know you have those days. Especially if you do not have support, you can just slide into negative habits like sliding into the wall.

Take a serious look at these habits that could be making depression worse:

1. What are you thinking about? Do you think about your failures, your weaknesses, and what you don't have? Are you thinking about what others have in material possessions, finances, health, relationships, job, or talents? Are you focused on your losses? Change your negative thinking. If you are telling yourself that you are a loser or are unlovable, then you are feeding your depression dinosaur. Dinosaurs could eat 40,000 calories a day! You have to challenge the negative thinking so you feel more positive and thus act more positively. Stop going over and over again where life went wrong. Habits need time to change but at least be aware of it. Journal it to catch yourself. Distracting yourself and meditation/prayer help.

2. What are you eating? Do you binge eat? If the depressed person has a diet with a lot of sugar, processed foods, refined grains, and fats, then it will make depression worse. There are several reports out there that depression is one of the symptoms of people with celiac disease or gluten sensitivity. This is due to intestinal damage that precludes the absorption of certain nutrients that are important for brain function. That delicious chocolate cake will cause a mood crash. When I've had a tough day, I love to get a brownie, but I consider what

that would look like to my weight and energy fluctuations if that were my habit.

3. Comfort foods can be deceptive. People look for that soda, pizza, hamburger, ice cream, chips, or macaroni and cheese. Can you skip the fries? The body looks for extra calories during times of stress. Really, not too many people want yogurt when they can have chocolate. Life must have balance, especially when depressed. It is not about depriving oneself but finding balance.

4. Are you getting the right amount of sleep? Do you stay in bed all day? The opposite would be not getting enough sleep, as depression causes sleep to be fitful. Be consistent with sleep times. It is recommended to turn off electronic devices thirty minutes to one hour before bed. This is because the blue light emitted from electronic gadgets negatively affects melatonin, which helps one sleep. You must get up at regular times even if you don't want to face the world.

5. Are you hanging with toxic people? They are people who are not supportive and are manipulating you, controlling you, and upsetting you. How will you feel better if you are with people who criticize you, pay no attention to your boundaries, and cause you grief and stress? Gees. Melancholy Melvin cannot feel better hanging with Toxic Tonya or Manipulative Mannie. Ask yourself how these people make you feel. Don't get sucked in; say "no" to these relationships and put yourself first.

6. Are you isolating yourself? Having contact with others who are stable helps one feel more stable. Loneliness can lead to depression, anxiety, and a potential risk of suicide. It does take energy to get out and be with others. Make every effort to accept dinner and activity invitations, and connect by calls, texts, and emails. Cut off being cut off!

7. Are you ignoring your hygiene? Are your clothes unclean and your home a mess? Have you stopped exer-

cising? I know that exercise sounds like extra fries, and that sounds better. Set timers and write yourself notes and ask others who care about you to help.

8. Many people do not realize that their hunched-over posture and their head down are keeping depression going. If you stand up straight and put your head up, it creates a generally optimistic outlook. It creates confidence and energy as well. Back, neck, and shoulder pain may be eliminated. Try posture-improving exercises and moving around more often if mobility allows you. Have books and televisions at an angle so as to not have to look down.

9. If you have low self-esteem or are an overly self-critical person, you are likely keeping depression going. List what you are good at. There are many resources out there to develop a happier you.

10. Are you drinking and drugging to drown or escape your woes? Alcohol is a depressant, even though you may not think so. That seemingly happy bar scene is a counterfeit to what you can have without the risk of addiction. Alcohol and drugs affect the chemistry of the brain. The depressants slow down the central nervous system. Once you drink over 0.08 mg/l, the depressant effects take over. With drugs you have stimulants as well as depressant drugs. That is another whole big ball of wax.

11. Are you wearing clothes that coordinate with your mood? For instance, grey is known as a dull, sad, and lonely color. No haters here; you can love it; I love it, but be careful what you wear on Dominick Downer days. Are you wearing the same clothes for days in a row? What you wear affects your level of confidence. Choose to dress for happiness. Consider yellow, green, or blue.

Isaiah 64:8b (NIV), "We are the clay, You are the potter; we are all the work of Your hand."

God makes and shapes us to be useful vessels and vessels of honor. If there are places where we don't look like that, then give it all to God, who knows how to fix us where we are broken.

Response:

_____

_____

_____

_____

_____

_____

_____

_____

_____

_____

_____

_____

_____

_____

_____

_____

The Tale of Two Turtles

"Animals are such agreeable friends-they ask no questions-they pass no criticism" (George Eliot).

This is the story of two turtles and how that relates to depression. Thomas Tribulation Turtle was having a really bad day and flipped over with no ability on his own to right himself back up. Along came a friend, Timothy Timely Turtle, who rather nicely rammed his friend back into his natural upright state. I actually had to watch this on YouTube to see for myself (https://www.youtube.com/watch?v=SEM2ZY1-RPc). Staying flipped over too long can cause dehydration and then death.

As you may have figured out, depressed people need others—a helping hand, or in Thomas Tribulation Turtle's case, a helping beak. I know I stretched this, but try to see the point. Support and encouragement are a must for recovery. You may just be the answer to help another regain hope and begin a path to enjoying life again. It may be a tricky endeavor, as there could be resistance. If it is you who has "flipped," please allow a helper in for a quicker recovery. Dehydration is serious, physically, emotionally, or spiritually.

That hard shell the turtle goes into is like the depressed person who is escaping into their "shell." The turtle does this escape behavior to protect itself, much like the depressed person is protecting themselves, intentionally or not. If they feel lonely, they will withdraw, and they "cover up" to hide the problem. Their self-esteem will take a hit as well due to their loss of interest in life. Their reclusive mood will likely push people away. It will become easy for them to say, "What's the use?" They often wonder if they will ever feel any differently. Encouragement is very much needed.

For a turtle that has retreated into its shell, a person may need to remove the environmental stressors before the turtle feels safe to come out. That may include dogs, cats, or loud room noises. People are much the same way. Conversely, people who are depressed may need their space. Maybe they just need to know you are there, not trying to "fix" them but there with the power of your presence, the power of silence, or the power of listening to them.

Friends who are trying to help a depressed friend need to do so without judgment. We all know that, but it slips out when we don't understand why our friends or family act the way they do. We may just need to be a big ear and listen. No matter what a person's age is, we will never outgrow our need for true friendships. True-blue friends will be there for you through thick and thin. They will make you feel included, like you belong, which will decrease feelings of hopelessness.

Your buddies are happy for you when you succeed. I have a great friend who has told me she has to be the first to buy my book. One's self-worth increases with this type of relationship. When I had a hard day, I called upon one of my friends and asked if I could vent, and thus she sat down while I spilled my woes, and I was never hurried. My mates are so ready to pray for me and mine through life's challenges and concerns, such as surgeries, accidents, financial needs, stressors, and heartaches of about every kind. Well, you know there are many of those and more to come just because life can be, well, life. It has the potential to be very harsh and unpredictable. They pray and trust that I have a good outcome for all life's concerns, such as job interviews, vacations, in-law visits, or medical procedures. You will find your buddy available to meet tangible needs, such as walking the dog, giving you a ride when your car is in the shop, or dropping food at the door when sick.

Friends are there when grief strikes. They have attended my family's funerals and vice versa. My buddies are consoling and supportive. Friends make us happier, which may translate to us living longer. They are trustworthy, loyal, and dependable and bring fun into an otherwise boring or depressive day. Pets and besties are truly major depression busters. Make sure the relationship of help and support is reciprocal.

Skills to try:

1. Let God into your heartache. Why would you not allow the One who has all the resources not to be there for you, especially when God loves you and longs to see you through and can do so perfectly? It can be futile without divine intervention. God's faithfulness is a guarantee.

2. Ask yourself, "Why do I feel stuck?" or "Why am I isolating myself?" Are there any areas you may be self-sabotaging? Are there any areas where doubt is plaguing you? Are you carrying any offense? Do you feel like you have self-worth? Is confidence waning? Do you have any issues with your level of energy or drive? If so, list the changes you want to make to "right yourself back up" and the plan to accomplish that.

3. Welcome positive people into your day and actually your life. Whether feeling stuck or wounded, people can get you going again. They can bring comfort and encouragement and are a brace when you are "belly up." They can help you see more clearly and be able to assist with practical things that are overwhelming. Please allow a trusting and wise person to help you "stick your neck out of your shell."

Ecclesiastes 4:9–10 (NIV), "Two are better than one, because they have a good return for their work. If one falls down, his friend

68

can help him up."

Two are definitely better than one. I wish you a Timothy Timely Turtle friend.

Response:

_____

_____

_____

_____

_____

_____

_____

_____

_____

_____

_____

_____

_____

_____

_____

_____

The Black Cloud

I am not sure if you think the title refers to an ominous, angry, gray cloud or something oppressive. Well, it is about something that happened to me many years ago. I knocked on the door of the leader's home to attend a Bible study, and someone answered the door and informed me that I had a black cloud over my head, figuratively, of course. Well, I was going through a very rough patch and was depressed but did not want my depression to be so obvious.

Black clouds are indicators of bad weather. The water droplets inside are getting heavy enough to begin falling. The cloud is dark because the light is not passing through. That was like me; there were heavy things happening, and I needed more "light" to pass through. I was walking with the Lord, so I had my best resource, but I still felt downhearted. Many people helped with tangible things and with prayer support. Understand that Christians are just like anybody else, and they can get depressed. We are not exempt. My faith was intact, and I still kept up with my spiritual disciplines. However, I was experiencing life in the form of serious trials, and it manifested in me as depression. I was tired but not weak. I was overwhelmed but not "down for the count." I was disheartened, but I had hope. For me, I just wanted to stop feeling the gloominess like a dark cloudy day.

On the flip side, who ever said that the struggles we want to end immediately will? If you can relate, then I encourage you that we both believe in the fact that prayer works and that God can do exceedingly above all that we ask or think. I did see the miracles happen little by little. God worked in and through and for me with His mysterious ways. It left me with such gratitude at the ways He was present, providing, powerful, preserving, and patient. I use those five "P" words, as maybe they fit your experience as well and they will help you remember God comes through for us sooner or later, but He always will.

Depression is an emotion that makes one feel like they are in a deep hole. It can be debilitating and overwhelming. It affects an individual's spirit, soul, and body. It affects one's energy, sleep, appetite, relationships, and ability to concentrate.

Know this: The Bible does not use the word "depression" per se but uses the phrase "The soul cast down" (Psalms 42 and 43). The Bible refers to "downcast" as "low in spirit" or "downhearted." The thesaurus states "downcast" can mean "forlorn, dejected, despondent, brokenhearted, miserable, dispirited, crushed, and grief-stricken," and those are only a few of the many synonyms. But you can learn from the next few pages some skills that you can put in your fanny pack and have near.

Depression is not God's will. It is not part of one's birthright in Christ. It is not a weakness or a flaw. It is not all in your head. It is not about being lazy, negative, or having a bad attitude. It is an illness. It is also not a joke. It is about people suffering.

Skills to try:

1. Talk about your feelings to an understanding, trusting person or professional. Talking takes strength, vulnerability, and courage. Do not isolate yourself.
2. Distract yourself and find something to do that makes you feel better.
3. Accept your condition, but seek treatment. It is treatable. You are not your illness. You are so much more. For example, you are not "bipolar"; you have bipolar disorder.

4. Consider educating others who may need to learn about the illness.

5. List ways you can empower your own life. Have no shame! Don't allow others to choose how you should view yourself. Tell yourself you have a mental illness, but you can and will live a meaningful life. You can make a difference.

6. Reach out to others. Pay forward. You know what it is like to be down and out, so see if there is something you can do for others. Hugs and smiles are free, and so is listening. Coffee with a friend does not cost much.

7. Have no stigma! Refute it totally.

8. Have persistence and courage. Be productive.

9. Don't neglect your spiritual side. God is near to the broken-hearted. Your journey through hardship is worse without God's intervention and constant love.

10. Call on professionals if you need help.

Third John 2 (NKJV), "Beloved, I wish above all things that you prosper and be in health even as your soul prospers."

God wants us to prosper, be complete and whole, and our soul to grow and thrive.

Response:

Change Your Cloud Color

In the previous page, I talked about my black cloud. Well, you must know how to change a dark cloud to a fluffy white cloud. Despair can be turned into hope. It is an absolute with some work. Keeping hope will send depression to the abyss (bottomless pit). Hope is your parachute through the dark clouds of despair. Hope is a desire for things to change for the better. Spiritually, it means good things will happen with faith in God. Dr. Valerie Maholmes from the American Psychology Association writes that hope is "planning, motivation and determination to get what one hopes for."

So let's get busy with the planning, motivation, and determination. First, get the mentality that you are worthy of being whole and living a life of joy. Second, you need to know that the deep hole you are in—you can climb out of it. I love the story of the farmer whose donkey fell in a hole, and the farmer felt like he had no choice but to just bury him. He shoveled dirt into the hole, but with every shovel of dirt, the donkey stepped up onto it and climbed his way out. Picture it. Third, you need to know that even though you feel alone, down deep inside you probably know you need help and encouragement. Accept it. The Lord is the light in all our darkness. His eyes are to and fro over all the face of the earth (2 Chronicles 16:9), and that includes deep holes. Do not keep the address of Pat Pitiful on 123 Pithole Lane, Poorthing, PA. How about the address Annie Anticipation on 777 Awaiting Road, Achievement, AZ? What address would you give to a more hopeful you?

A white cloud is a cloud of random scattering white light from the sun that includes small water droplets or ice crystals. Clouds in the Old Testament days symbolized the presence of God. When the people of Israel were being led out of Egypt, it was by a pillar of cloud by day to guide them (Exodus 13:21). This cloud protected them from forty years of the scorching sun they were about to endure and possibly from enemies.

In Exodus 24:16–18 Moses climbed up Mount Sinai. The glory of the Lord was in the cloud covering the mountain. For six days the cloud covered the mountain, and on the seventh day, the Lord called to Moses from within the cloud. Moses entered the cloud, and it is recorded that he stayed on the mountain for forty days and forty nights. It was here that Moses received the Ten Commandments.

It was also recorded that a cloud filled the tent of meeting with His presence. In Exodus 33:7–11 Moses pitched a "tent of meeting" outside of camp. When Moses went into the tent, the pillar of cloud came down and stayed at the entrance while the Lord spoke with Moses while in the cloud. The Lord would speak to Moses face to face as a man speaks with his friend. This is a wonderful description of Moses and God talking like one would talk to a friend. But Moses did not actually see God, as it is written in John 14:9 that no man has seen God. Still, having the amazing experience of chatting with God, whether through a cloud or a burning bush, had to have been way over the top of extraordinary moments.

When you see clouds today, consider thinking the same way— that they are a symbol of His presence. I will also call His presence in our life the number one way to dispel darkness.

Examine what things could be smothering your hope. Do you have a negative mindset? Are you isolating yourself? Are Negative Neil or Defeatist Della your support system? Did you discontinue your positive habits, such as keeping a routine, eating right, getting enough sleep, and exercising? If you made goals, did you give up on them? Is doubt plaguing you?

Skills to try:

1. Give up denial and pride. How will you make any progress if you are still trying to hide your condition? I did not admit my depression because that would have meant something was wrong. For an odd explanation, that meant to me that I was inadequate or less in some way.

2. Stop any negative thinking! Picture a big red stop sign every time you tell yourself something like, "You are never getting out of this hole." Change it to "I can do this one step at a time or one day at a time."

3. Do not berate yourself. Life can be two steps up and one step down the ladder. Self-compassion is helpful to your recovery.

4. Write down your plans on how you will not just survive but thrive, even if it is hard to see that happening. Make them realistic.

5. Break out of all the bad habits. Take responsibility for your negative learned behavior.

6. Engage in pleasurable activities regularly.

Psalm 46:1 (NIV), "God is our refuge and strength, an ever-present help in trouble."

Sounds like a promise and has hope all over it.

Response:

_____

_____

_____

_____

_____

_____

_____

_____

_____

_____

_____

_____

_____

_____

_____

_____

_____

_____

_____

_____

_____

_____

Evict the Bad Guest

Everybody and their dog "Bennie Bedhog" and their cat "Haddie Hairball" will be sad at times. Sadness is not depression. We can be sad to know our friend has health problems or we are short on money for vacation. Sadness does not last. Depression seems to go on; staying for breakfast, lunch, and dinner and spending the night too. Put out the eviction sign! Sometimes a person can't get rid of that nightmare of a guest (depression) due to their depressive thinking. Depressive thoughts are inaccurate, unfair, and unrealistic. Depressive thoughts, cognitive distortions, or faulty thinking, whichever you want to call them, need to be replaced with positive, truthful ones.

Here are the ten most common distortions:

1. *Catastrophizing*—a small thing becomes a disaster. Example: somebody was going to call you, but they didn't, so you think the worst has happened to them.

2. *All-or-nothing thinking*—you see things in extremes, no middle ground. Example: people or situations are either great or terrible.

3. *Discounting the positive*—good things happen, but you focus on the negative. Example: you had a good interview, but you focused on one thing you may have said wrong.

4. *Overgeneralization*—you overgeneralize one life event into another. Example: One relationship of yours failed, so you expect all your relationships will fail.

5. *Labeling*—you define and talk to yourself with negative labels. You tell yourself you are stupid, ugly, or a loser. Example: you gained some weight, so you tell yourself you are fat.

6. *Filtering*—you only see the bad, not the good. You see your life and future negatively. You ignore anything positive. Example: a person says a kind thing to you, and the next one says a rude comment, so you believe there are only rude people out there.

7. *Mind-reading*—you think you know what others think about you and that it is always negative. You jump to conclusions. Your significant other had a bad day, and it caused them to be late coming home. You assumed you could read their mind, and you reacted instead of asking.

8. *Personalization*—you take things too personally. You blame yourself for things outside of your control. Example: your child got a bad grade in school, so you believe it is your fault.

9. *"Should" statements*—you have a list of rules of how people should and shouldn't behave. You blame yourself or others for what should or shouldn't have been said or done. Example: I should lose weight before I start dating again.

10. *Emotional reasoning*—you rely on your gut instead of evidence. Example: I feel unattractive; therefore, I must be unattractive.

So distorted thinking may have been with you for years, so it is a habit. It will take a while for you to master a healthier way of thinking.

Skill to try:

1. For a week write down every time you catch yourself thinking any of the above. Work on how you can stop the erroneous thinking.

Romans 12:2 (NIV), "Do not conform any longer to the pattern of this world, but be transformed by the renewing of your mind."

Do not be part of the world's thinking that is devoid of God.

What consumes your mind will control you. Renew your mind to the things of the Spirit, and you will experience more joyful living.

Response:

_____

_____

_____

_____

_____

_____

_____

_____

_____

_____

_____

_____

_____

_____

_____

_____

The Saboteur

A saboteur is a person who commits sabotage, which means they undermine a cause. The cause in this case is threatening recovery from depression. There was a time that was me, as I had a good case of self-pity. Maybe you do now. Seriously, I think most, if not all of us, have felt a bit sorry for ourselves at some time in life. Well, at least look at the circumstances and if you see possibilities of any self-pity, then call mutiny on yourself.

Self-pity, defined by the *Oxford Dictionary*, is "excessive, self-absorbed unhappiness over one's own troubles." I don't think I liked that definition when I was struggling, but the truth is it is a self-focus. It comes across where we feel a sense of lack or "poor me." We must quit looking inside of ourselves and quit looking around at others. When a person has the pain of emotional distress and things have gone south, there is a tendency for other people who do not understand to look at them and think they should "snap out of it." This is not fair or helpful. We never know what others have gone through, and we should never minimize their distress. I read this somewhere, and it is worth repeating without me knowing the source, "Don't look down on someone unless you are doing so to pick them up."

However, nothing produces depression or keeps one in depression longer than self-pity. Also, it is not helpful in overcoming depression to keep the "why me syndrome." This thinking pattern needs to stop so you can heal. You have to reject the voices that come at you and try to tell you, "You deserve this bad treatment" or "You will never have anything good happen to you, so don't expect it." Use caution around people who reject you, insult you, or injure you. Protect the space around you, and don't allow Naomi Naysayer or Karl Killjoy in that space. They are negative and critical.

Moses in Numbers 11:10–15 (NIV) had self-pity, anger, and resentment. He addressed God with his six complaints and questions and ended up saying, "If this is how you are going to treat me, put me to death right now—if I have found favor in your eyes—do not let me face my own ruin." My first thought was, *What is up with you?* However, we can't minimize what one may be going through. A huge number of people were complaining and crying at Moses, and like life, he needed help. His burden was very great. The question could be asked, "Did he call on God to help him?" His best resource, God, was right there. Did his self-pity overtake him for a moment? He is human like us; it happens. God came to him with help in the form of seventy elders.

God will not come down and do your living for you. There is work to do to give up self-pity and stay free from it. Remember self-pity will maximize your difficulties. It will destroy any motivation you have, and it will make you feel stuck. Look at it as something that will ruin your life and something that will make you feel without hope and fragmented. Say goodbye to it.

Skills to try:

1. For some of you who feel like self-pity is a sin, then confess it and ask forgiveness. Ask God to step into your circumstance and take you through it.

2. Become self-aware of your feelings and change your perspective. Hardships can cause a person to grow stronger. I certainly was very determined I was not going down with the ship. Develop gumption.

3. Question wrong thinking.

4. Is your outlook realistic? Maybe things are not as bad as

you think. Look for the good.

5. Change the picture of how you see yourself. Don't consider yourself a victim. Don't look around and think you have it worse than others.

6. What can you do to get busy and make the changes that need to be made? If it can't be changed, then accept the situation. People will get sick and die, a storm will come, and children will leave when you know it is not a good idea. At the same time, your car may break down, and you have four bills due when you only have enough money to pay two of the bills, or you have two dollars but wish you could put more gas than that in your car. Now you must get resourceful. Get your trusty support group to help. Friends, family, and church would normally put gas in your car if they could and if they knew.

7. Express gratitude. This is very important. You can't be pitiful and powerful at the same time. Don't we actually have much to be grateful for anyway? I have a roof over my head, a vehicle to drive, clothes and shoes, great family and friends, health, the fresh air to breathe, and I can see, hear, walk, and talk. My cupboard is full. I am loved. I always find it helpful to express out loud or on paper the many things I can appreciate. These expressions chase the "sorry side of our life" down the road to a deep ditch. There are many out there who have little to nothing. My son went on a mission trip and came back with stories of terrible poverty he witnessed. We are blessed even though we are experiencing much trouble.

Psalm 71:20 (NIV), "Though You have made me see trouble, many and bitter, You will restore my life again; from the depths of the earth, You will again bring me up."

That's God; He is a restorer.

Response:

_____

_____

_____

_____

_____

_____

_____

_____

_____

_____

_____

_____

_____

_____

_____

_____

_____

_____

_____

Disabilities and Inspiration

The golden rule applies to the person with a disability. Treat that person as you would want to be treated. However, ask the person before you jump in to help. It is benevolent on your part to want to help, but it may be something the person with the disability can do for themself and wants to do. Do not patronize that person or show pity. That could be diminishing or insulting. Respect their choices. Include that person in activities when possible. When you encounter someone who has a disability, see them as a person first. Ask about them without it becoming nosiness but as an effort to get to know them. After you get to know the person with a disability, you may have developed a relationship enough to maybe encourage them to connect with others who have similar challenges, like being part of a disability support group. There would be a common bond and understanding, and likely they would less feeling self-conscious. Respect their choice to not join anything as well.

For the person who has a diagnosis, physical or mental or both, you may need to grieve that you have a change that happened to you and will need to process that. Your feelings will run the gamut, which is normal. You have never had limitations like you do now, so have patience with yourself. You will need to make new goals. Nurturing yourself is very important. Be sure to set your home environment up for your comfort. Keep in the forefront of your mind that in spite of changes you have gone through, you have a purpose, even if it takes you some time to reevaluate what that is.

"I can be changed by what happens to me. But I refuse to be reduced by it" (Maya Angelou).

"We are put in situations to build our character, not to destroy us" (Nick Vujicic, Life without Limbs).

"Hard things are put in our way, not to stop us, but to call out our courage and strength" (Unknown).

"I have a disability, yes, that is true, but all that means is I may have to take a slightly different path than you" (Robert M. Hensel, born with spina bifida).

I want to give honor and thanks to three participants who graciously allowed me to interview them in order for the readers to find inspiration in the story of their disability. Here is the interview.

What kind of disability do you have?

SN. I have schizoaffective disorder, and my spine has an inoperable cyst, which affects my mobility.

SK. I have neuropathy, nerve damage, hyperactive nerves, back pain, mobility issues, and will use a walker the rest of my life.

JE. I have chronic pain, heart disease, arthritis, and diabetes.

Do you have any mental health issues because of your disabilities?

SN. I have anxiety and sometimes depression.

SK. I have depression sometimes. I get frustrated due to the things I can't do. I have insomnia.

JE. Depression, of course, and my memory is not like it used to be. I have insomnia.

How are your activities of daily living affected by your disability? What are you not doing?

SN. They are limited. Mostly I don't go any further than the porch. I don't walk.

SK. Everything is affected. Showering and dressing have been challenging. I can't scrub and vacuum. I can't lift. Somebody has to get the groceries for me. It is frustrating.

JE. I can't do what I used to do. Pain has robbed me of energy. I can't seem to look ahead. I am not exercising, not walking, and not playing with the grandkids. I am not enjoying life.

What is your hardest challenge?

SN. Just living life. Getting up in the morning is hard.

SK. It is walking due to my balance issues.

JE. Getting up to start my day is difficult. It takes two cups of coffee and meds to kick in.

How do you feel like people perceive you?

SN. Childlike, like I am stuck at the age my disability was diagnosed.

SK. Nobody looks at me any differently.

JE. Like a trooper because I keep on keeping on. I feel down inside, but I don't act like it. I press on regardless.

What coping skills have you tried? Which ones worked and which did not work?

SN. Prayer works. Watching YouTube works. Group worked. Regular therapy did not work.

SK. Keeping a positive outlook, having a dog, and having visitors help. I use the iPad, watch TV, stay busy, and entertain myself.

JE. God, definitely. I ask God to help me make it, and He does. I distract myself by watching movies. I must take my meds. I sing, and I don't focus on my pain when I do that.

Singing makes endorphins work.

Do you know your purpose?

SN. I will try and discover that after I get healed, but I want to minister to other people.

SK. I love life even with my pain issues. I feel like I have a lot to give and offer family and friends. I enjoy taking care of others in many different ways as long as I am capable of doing what they need. I love spending time with my children, grandchildren, and other family and friends. I love nature and what the world has to offer. I am very thankful for what God has given me.

JE. My purpose would be finding and doing God's will for my life.

Is there anything else you would like to add to help someone who is going through similar challenges?

SN. Stay with it and have courage.

SK. Be patient and stay positive. Keep a good outlook on life.

JE. I found that singing brings joy to others as well. Help your children out when you can.

Skill to try:

1. What speaks to you from these brave interviewees? Are there any adjustments you can adopt for yourself? For example, they gave ideas for coping skills and keeping a positive attitude.

Philippians 4:11 (NIV), "I am not saying this because I am in need, for I have learned to be content whatever the circumstance."

As hard as this will sound, don't let the outside circumstance determine your inner life. The apostle Paul drew on the reservoir inside of him (the Lord). He did not allow what was happening to him to disturb his faith. He felt like there was nothing he could not face, as he had the Lord.

Response:

_____

_____

_____

_____

_____

_____

_____

_____

_____

_____

_____

_____

_____

_____

_____

_____

_____

_____

_____

_____

Eunice and Jonathan

Eunice was the little-known mother of Timothy in the Bible. She raised Timothy so well that the apostle Paul was able to use him greatly in the ministry. She was very devoted to him, prayed for him, and taught him well. Jonathan was King David's best friend. This was a very strong bond, the likes of which many people never experience. Jonathan was selfless, very loyal, and loved his friend greatly and vice versa. He even warned him when his father wanted to kill him.

So what does this have to do with depression? Eunice was family, and Jonathan was a friend. The depressed person needs this kind of support to move from depression to happiness. As a family member or a friend, you may have been frustrated at attempts to help. You may have offered support, and it was rejected, or you didn't offer any and were accused of not caring. These coping skills and suggestions are for you:

1. Watch your responses—do not tell the depressed person to "get a grip" or "snap out of it." They will feel aggravated, as they are in a struggle. Offer something better, something that will help them recover, such as "You will get through this." Or "You can do this, and I will be there to help you."

2. Be a good listener—people talk to those who they feel can be trusted, so be trustworthy and keep their confidence unless there is a risk of self-harm or harm to others. The depressed person often wonders if anybody cares, so active listening is key to them not feeling rejected.

3. Be there—your presence is evidence that you care. Don't probe. Maybe you don't even need to talk. Offer compassion, comfort, and hope. If there was a time

when you were in despair, you can tell how God brought you through. Do not make up anything just to try and relate.

4. Do not feel sorry for your family or friends. Weep with those who weep (Romans 12:15b). Don't condemn them, and do not offer pity. Pity can make another feel insulted or humiliated and that you are looking down on them. Offer compassion, which is having a feeling of "suffering together" and wanting to do something to help.

5. Don't rush the unhappy person. If it is very clear to you what needs to be done, that does not mean they are ready to hear it or do it. They may need to come to their own conclusions. They may even think you forced your plan on them. You cannot dictate how another person should feel.

6. If you can, get them moving. Action is an antidote for despondency. Physical activity will stimulate the chemicals in the brain that help one feel better. Just start with one activity a day. The hard part is to get them started, as they are generally passive. Encourage them to keep a routine.

7. Do not judge. Don't even allow judgmental grimaces to cross your face. Instead, ask, "What can I do to lift the burden?"

8. Encourage your friend or loved one to avoid caffeine, alcohol, and sugar and to take B vitamins. The body needs special attention when it is down in the dumps. You will find the depressed person does not eat correctly—eats too much, not at all, or mostly the wrong foods.

9. It is important for the depressed person to get out of the house. It is especially beneficial for them to be outdoors between 11:00 a.m. and 2:00 p.m., as the sun acts as an antidepressant. It increases one's serotonin, which will also help keep seasonal affective disorder at bay. Getting your person out to a favorite place is extra nice.

10. Encourage your friend or family member to keep a routine, such as getting up in the morning. They may not have slept well, and they may be trying to sleep their problems away. Anxiety and dread may be the norm for their start of the day. Making an activity list might help keep the momentum going.

11. Do not compare the person you are trying to help with somebody else. Hannah Happy may not have had the challenges of Charlie Cheerless. Hannah Happy might have learned coping skills and had a lot of support, whereas Charlie Cheerless has had one thing after another go wrong. Charlie feels like nobody has been there for him, and his attitude about life is, "It will not get better." The devil likes to point out the advantages others have, especially when that one has a heavy heart. It does not help if you say, "Why can't he or she just do this or that like their sister?" Comparisons hurt. Find the fine line between helping appropriately and minding your own business.

12. A hug relieves stress. It boosts the mood. Cuddling with a pet is a great mood elevator. Walking a dog gets one out and encountering nature and neighbors. Touch, in general, causes our body to release the "feel good" hormones. Research reports hugging may even reduce pain. Hugging may not take the heartache away, but it will be a source of comfort and communicate that you care.

Philippians 2:4 (NIV), "Each of you should look not only to your own interests, but also to the interests of others."

We are to take care of ourselves, but be kind, considerate, and helpful to others.

Response:

_____

_____

_____

_____

_____

_____

_____

_____

_____

_____

_____

_____

_____

_____

_____

_____

_____

_____

_____

_____

_____

Joseph and Elizabeth Are Also Helpers

Jesus, of course, is the son of God, but did you think what it might have been like for Joseph to raise a child who was not his own as well as one with such an enormous, holy calling? He did raise Jesus as his own, and we do not know much, except he was a righteous man and taught carpentry to Jesus. He must have taken the job of fatherhood seriously. Elizabeth was the mother of John the Baptist. She dedicated her son to the Lord. She was pregnant with the "prophet who would prepare the way of the Lord." Again, this is a serious responsibility for her to raise him for his special calling.

Here are more skills to consider from the previous pages to help a depressed person:

1. Give hope and consolation—we can be comforters. It is a good feeling to help another. The doleful person has a negative outlook, and what little goals they had probably went down the toilet. They also think way too much about their failures and their so-called dismal future. Do not give your horror story but give a true story of hope that Christ is aware of their situation and has answers for them. Most of the time, depressed people have lost their spiritual footing. Consolation is comfort given at a time of disappointment, and hope is expectation with confidence. We all can do this.

2. Encourage them to spend time with family and friends— associations are important. Those who are with others fare better when they are in a community. Those relationships will likely be able to help with the heartache and loneliness. It does not work for them to be around depressed people. Depressed people can pass their bleak mood to others. Stable people make a good bond.

3. Encourage laughter—it will stimulate the endorphins.

Watch a funny movie together and tell some funny jokes or some antics from the past. Depressed people sometimes feel like they should not be laughing, as it feels odd to them to be enjoying something.

4. Pray—ask if you can pray with them. Pray for them when you are not with them as well. Do not allow any condemnation in your prayer. As they hear you pray with thanksgiving, it will be therapeutic for them to be reminded that God is near and so available. Encourage them to pray even if they tell you God does not hear or answer.

5. Encourage them a lot. The depressed person may think that any light at the end of the tunnel is a train coming to finish them off. They are busy assuming the worst. Remind your person that when God is in the picture, anything is possible.

6. Always point them to the Lord—He loves, listens, and rescues, and all of heaven's resources are at His disposal for solutions. They will need to learn to get their needs met from the Lord. In this way, they can develop a relationship that will sustain them all their life.

7. Use the Word of God—ask God what scripture you can pray for them and what wisdom you can use to speak to them. Be aware they could have resentment toward God. There may be a multitude of great counselors, but His Word is supernatural and effective for overcoming depression.

8. Be patient with them, as normal tasks and responsibilities take longer for them to accomplish. They may even go a significant amount of time not doing anything. Depression drains one's energy; the less energy you have, the more depressed you feel.

9. Be aware that physical pain and depression are cousins that feed off of each other. Disabilities and other physical challenges can bring on depression, and depression can bring on pain.

10. Do not try and convince them that they should "at least be positive." This causes added frustration and anxiety to add to their already low mood. If you are being Chelsea Cheerful while they are in emotional pain, they may want you to depart from them, as all that cheeriness can be annoying. Be sensitive to the fact that depression has taken over every part of their life, and it magnifies every thought and feeling. Your overly happy self is just too much. It reminds them again that they don't feel normal and that they are missing happiness.

11. Take all threats of suicide seriously.

Proverbs 11:25 (NIV), "A generous man will prosper; he who refreshes others will himself be refreshed."

God is pleased when we lovingly serve others. Being charitable has its own reward. Just be there for your depressed person.

Response:

_____

_____

_____

_____

_____

_____

_____

_____

_____

_____

_____

_____

_____

_____

_____

_____

_____

_____

_____

_____

More Serotonin, Less Cortisol

"The moment you change your perception is the moment you rewrite the chemistry of your body" (Dr. Bruce H. Lipton).

"When you start taking care of yourself, you start feeling better, you start looking better, and you even start to attract better, it all starts with you" (Unknown).

"Replace habits: movies and shows with sleep, fast food with home-made food, toxic friends with mentors, television with exercise, complaining with gratitude, overthinking with action, and blame with responsibility" (Unknown).

Before we can understand the next page on what foods help decrease depression and anxiety, there are some big words that will explain the whys of it all. Dive in.

Tryptophan (trip tuh fn)—an amino acid needed for normal growth in infants and for the production and maintenance of the body's proteins, muscles, enzymes, and neurotransmitters. Your body cannot produce this, so you must get it from your diet. This would be in milk, tuna, turkey, chicken, oats, cheese, nuts, and seeds.

Dopamine—a type of neurotransmitter. It plays a role in how we feel pleasure, satisfaction, and motivation. It regulates body movements. Low levels of dopamine are linked to reduced motivation and decreased enthusiasm for life. Eat lots of protein, eat less saturated fat, and consume probiotics. Exercise often to boost endorphins and improve mood. Get enough sleep, meditate/pray, and get a safe amount of sunlight.

Endorphins—a group of hormones secreted from the brain and nervous system. They have a lot of psychological functions. They are natural painkillers released by the hypothalamus and pituitary gland in response to pain and stress. They work to relieve pain and create a general feeling of well-being. Endorphins are produced during exercise, sex, laughing, dancing, and listening to music, to name a few. Foods that stimulate the release of endorphins are cacao, spicy foods, Rhodiola, ginseng, and vanilla bean. The scent of vanilla beans is a natural aphrodisiac, and it will also increase neurotransmitter function. It is an antioxidant and helps with inflammation.

Cortisol—when faced with a stressor, the adrenal glands secrete cortisol, which prepares the body for a fight-or-flight response. Ways to balance cortisol levels are to talk about your stress, say no when you need to, create more healthy relationships in your life, exercise regularly, and eat more nutrient-rich foods.

Serotonin—a chemical produced naturally in the nerve cells. It is a monoamine neurotransmitter made from the amino acid tryptophan. When serotonin levels are normal, you feel happy, calmer, and more focused. Low levels of serotonin may cause depression, anxiety, and insomnia. A doctor might prescribe a selective serotonin reuptake inhibitor (SSRI) to treat depression. What helps is sunshine, exercise, a healthy diet, and meditation/prayer. Note: serotonin is synthesized from tryptophan.

Skill to try:

1. From the above, what adjustments do you need to make? Find life balance.

First Corinthians 10:31 (NIV), "So, whether you eat or drink or whatever you do, do it all for the glory of God."

With the things you eat, drink, and do, can you say you are doing them for the glory of God?

Response:

_____

_____

_____

_____

_____

_____

_____

_____

_____

_____

_____

_____

_____

_____

_____

_____

_____

_____

Depressed Donald and Anxious Agnes

"Down in the Dumps" Donald does not seem to know why he is in a funky mood. But he just had two donuts for breakfast and fast food for lunch. He has had way too much caffeine. Anxious Agnes is feeling stressed. She usually skips breakfast. Alice gets to work and encounters a tray of bagels and has two of them with cream cheese for her lunch. She brings hot deli items home for dinner. To keep herself going, she had an energy drink.

Well-meaning people do not seem to be making the connection to what they eat or don't eat contributes to their mood. Eating a healthy diet will help one think more clearly, be more alert, feel less fatigued, and feel happier. The brain has neurotransmitters that play a big role in a person's mood. When a person is struggling with depression or anxiety, there is usually an imbalance in these.

Here is some food for thought (literally). These are some suggestions on what to eat to feel more relaxed and happier:

1. *Walnuts* are a source of omega fatty acids, antioxidants, and protein that helps reduce symptoms of anxiety and depression.
2. *Dark chocolate* contains tyrosine, which is linked to an increase of dopamine. It stimulates the pleasure centers of the brain. Don't mess up your pleasure center! It releases endorphins. For those with anxiety, it reduces cortisol levels.
3. *Blueberries* help reduce levels of stress and anxiety. Vitamin C helps lower cortisol.
4. *Avocados* can help you relax. They are high in protein, which will help with dopamine production.
5. *Spinach* has high levels of magnesium, which is the best mineral for anxiety. Spinach is a feel-good food.

6. *Fish* is brain food, so it boosts cognitive functioning. It has high levels of omega-3 fatty acids and is a source of tryptophan.

7. *Chickpeas* increase cognitive function and improve mood and sleep.

8. *Greek yogurt* can reduce depression and anxiety.

9. *Eggs* are high in vitamin B and protein, which helps improve depression as well as boost neurotransmitter levels.

10. *Bananas* contain Vitamin B6, which helps the body create serotonin.

11. *Sweet potatoes* are rich in magnesium, which helps reduce stress and anxiety.

12. *Whole grains*—many of them contain high levels of tryptophan.

13. Foods rich in antioxidants for depression are *pecans, goji berries, grapes, cranberries, cherries, apples*, and *artichokes*.

Those are nineteen foods listed to improve your mood and health.

What is so bad about Donald and Agnes's food choices? Cleveland Clinic reports donuts have fifteen to thirty grams of sugar in each donut. This causes the body to pump out loads of insulin to try and accommodate. A huge blood sugar spike will then lead to an even bigger sugar crash. The extreme up and down leaves you hungry soon after breakfast, and you'll crave even more refined carbs. It's a vicious cycle of unhealthy eating. About four cups of caffeine are safe for most healthy adults, per Mayo Clinic. However, caffeine is a stimulant, and too much in a day can cause a person to feel jittery and anxious. Donald's fast-food lunch was high in sugar, salt, saturated fat, trans fat, processed ingredients, and calories. It is generally low in nutrients. The pizza he took home to the kids for dinner is more unhealthy than healthy. It is high in calories, unhealthy fats, carbs, and sodium. With it being an American staple, just use moderation.

Agnes' two bagels with cream cheese are about 300–500 calories each of starch. More calories and saturated fats are added for the cream cheese. Diets high in refined carbohydrates have been linked to an increase in type 2 diabetes (Cleveland Clinic). If Agnes picked up rotisserie chicken, she made a good choice. If it was fried chicken that she picked up, then it's a protein, which is good, but it is full of calories and fat, and it's breaded and fried in oil. A diet full of greasy foods will take a toll on your health. Not sure how often Agnes has an energy drink, but excessive or regular consumption can lead to heart arrhythmias, headaches, high blood pressure, and anxiety (*Insider*, January 13, 2021).

Skill to try:

1. For one week write down all you eat and drink as well as what your mood is. See a pattern? Make healthier adjustments to your eating and to your drinking. Then write down again what you ate and drank and what your mood was after healthy eating.

First Corinthians 3:16 (NIV), "Don't you know that you yourselves are God's temple and that God's spirit lives in you?"

Our bodies belong to the Lord. How are you treating yours?

Response:

_____

_____

_____

_____

_____

_____

_____

_____

_____

_____

_____

_____

_____

_____

_____

_____

_____

_____

_____

It Takes a Village with Children

"It takes a village to raise a child" is an African proverb that means it takes many people (the village) to help a child feel safe, happy, and secure. Sadly, children do experience depression. The Center for Disease Control (CDC) reports from dates 2016–2019 in the US that 4.4 percent or 2.7 million children from ages three to seventeen were depressed. This section is to help the adults in their life know some skills to be helpful. Many children with depression may have another disorder along with it, such as anxiety or ADHD (attention deficit hyperactivity disorder). First and foremost, depression is complex, and an evaluation with a doctor may be necessary, as well as having case managers, therapists, teachers, coaches, and spiritual advisors involved.

Let's talk about that village. I was very pleased to have other people help with my three sons. Life had thrown some trauma our way, and I found myself quite in need. First of all, choose carefully who your "village people" will be. It was important that they were kind, wise, and safe and would fully consider my child's welfare. It just naturally flowed to have coaches, church members, family, neighbors, and friends. I was not scared to leave them when I had hand-chosen those I personally trusted. If you have anxiety, it may take you longer to do this. Unfortunately, from my years of working with the sheriff's department, there are those offenders who could cause great harm. Obviously, moms, dads, and guardians, only leave your children with highly trusted people.

Second, are you emotionally ready to have other reliable adults correct your child if needed? I was fine with a person reminding my child to use manners, look before crossing the street, share, and not hit. I was good with a coach telling my child how to "shake it off" with a call they didn't like on the ball field. It was acceptable for a teacher to tell my child that certain behaviors would not be tolerated in the classroom. I was also pleased that another adult taught my son how to develop empathy and never be a bully or laugh at the awkward new student. Reminders to my child to not take things without asking and to watch their mouth are totally beneficial. Don't you think that your child will grow up and learn to respect other people's opinions, ask before borrowing, apologize, not interrupt while others are speaking, and offer to help without being asked because of the positive influence of others? It's all about raising them in a safe and healthy environment where they can thrive.

Any parents or guardians that have depressed children usually feel the frustration, even hopelessness, of how to get their child help. Early childhood depression may affect brain development, so it is serious. Depression is a constant low feeling for a period of time, even many months. Parents need to be alert to the signs of depression in children. Some signs are loss of interest in activities, trouble concentrating or making decisions, feeling worthless and tired, sleep issues, appetite changes, changes in school performance, crying more easily, irritability, loneliness, feelings of being overwhelmed, and physical complaints.

One's village may have resources and ideas for helping. They might have gone through a similar experience with one of their own family members and can offer support and wise suggestions. It may be plausible that they are so understanding and educated about your child's condition that they know how to respond to lift the heavy mood and redirect if necessary.

Skills to try:

1. Set up a dialogue with your child to open lines of communication. Let your child know it is okay to be upset, that what they feel won't last forever, and that you are there for them.

2. Set up that initial doctor appointment and inform the doctor of the behavior changes.

3. Be present, be empathetic, and be patient.

4. Put some fun activities in their routine. Be in the sunshine with them more for the benefits.

5. Encourage good sleep habits and nutrition, physical activity, and hygiene.

6. Learn and teach problem-solving skills to your child and how to regulate their own emotions. Teach your child how to be resilient and how to deal with tough life situations. There is a section in this book for that. These skills will go far as an adult.

7. Encourage social connections, such as time with family and friends, attending church, sports, clubs, scouts, music practice, etcetera. Counteract any resistance.

8. Recovery takes time, and there may be setbacks. Do your part if there has been a trauma or major life change to get through it successfully yourself. Model a healthy life so they see hope.

9. Choose village helpers carefully. Be a village member for others and teach your child about assisting others. It is full of benefits.

An important number to have on hand is the suicide prevention hotline at 800–273–8255.

Luke 18:16 (NIV), "Let the children come to me, and do not hinder them for the kingdom of God belongs to such as these."

Jesus wanted the children to come to Him, and He wanted to bless them.

Response:

_____

_____

_____

_____

_____

_____

_____

_____

_____

_____

_____

_____

_____

_____

_____

_____

_____

_____

_____

_____

_____

The Village Needs to Be Okay

Sometimes parents deny that their child is chronically unhappy, and sometimes it is a case of "I don't know what to do." Parents find themselves feeling overwhelmed, fearful, anxious, worried, and guilty with the tasks of doing the right thing to care for a depressed child along with their other responsibilities. The parent must remember that a child has little to no control in their life and has limited coping skills. The child's brain is still developing, and where there is confusion, they lose their sense of self. The depressed child may not have the verbal skills to express their feelings.

Things that parents need to understand are whether or not some of the child's depression is from a trauma, chronic illness, a conduct or learning disorder, verbal, emotional, or physical abuse or neglect, peer pressure, or a loss, to name a few. Parents must ask themselves if their parenting is inconsistent or if the home life is stressful. Are there any new events, such as getting a new step-parent or step-siblings or a death? Important considerations are whether or not the child is getting affection and positive feedback. Possibly the stress from poor economic conditions is a factor. In general are there any poor relationships? Does the child feel wanted and loved? Does anyone help with homework? Do you have playtime together? Does the parent attend any of the child's school or extracurricular activities and give positive feedback? A child feeling helpless can lead to despair.

Ask your child some pertinent questions, such as:

Are you anxious or worried about anything? When you are sad, what makes you feel better? Do you feel tired, bored, or afraid? If so, why do you feel that way? Do you have anybody in your life that has been picking on you? Do you feel like quitting or giving up on anything?

Skills to try:

1. Your reasoning is not your child's reasoning—the child may think life events were caused by them. They are egocentric (they think whatever happens relates to them). Preteens can usually see the viewpoint of others.

2. Give love and affection—lack of love and affection is a precursor to depression. This will set them up to be resentful and have self-pity.

3. Shower them with acceptance—sometimes children think they were a mistake. If a parent is rejecting a child and maybe the parent does not know they are doing that, then it could be that there is a trait in the child that reminds them of themself or someone that they do not care for.

4. Openly display appropriate parental love—a child who sees his parents love each other will develop a predisposition toward security and a healthy mental attitude.

5. Disciple wisely and fairly—children are not perfect. Children with depression may need a different approach. They need understandable and special rules. Disciple their behavior, not their emotions. Teach them how to deal with feelings like anger and embarrassment. Be consistent.

6. Don't be that parent who is full of criticism, condemnation, or griping or would humiliate their child. Guard against voicing your own negativity or defeatism. Don't express your own self-pity. Break any patterns of perfectionism, as children who think they have to be perfect are at a high risk of having depression and anxiety. Dissatisfied parents create a controlling home life.

First Corinthians 13:4–8 (NIV):

> *Love is patient, love is kind; It does not envy; it does not boast, it is not proud. It is not rude, it is not self-seeking. It is not easily angered, it keeps no record of wrongs. Love does not delight in evil but rejoices with the truth. It always protects, always trusts, always hopes, and always perseveres. Love never fails.*

This is a love that forgives and reaches out to others sacrificially. This is the nature of Christ.

Response:

_____

_____

_____

_____

_____

_____

_____

_____

_____

_____

_____

_____

It Takes a Village with Teenagers as Well

Picture yourself as a teenager, full of hormones and feeling awkward in almost every way. Now, add no social support because your family turned against you and actually plotted to do away with you. Other people turned against you as well. You feel very alone. You have been arrested, beaten, ridiculed, and called a liar. To top it off, you were thrown into a well to starve to death. Everything about your life seems to be cruel and solitary without support, and you are so young! Nobody listens to you. You are also aware you will never marry.

Who do you think is this mystery person? Joseph? Someone who suffered with leprosy? The tax collector? Daniel? Samson? The answer is Jeremiah. He is being highlighted because he was a teenager when God called him at a young age. God told him He had a plan for him before he was born that he would be set apart for the nation (Jeremiah 1:5). Jeremiah's response was, "Ah, sovereign Lord…I do not know how to speak; I am only a child" (Jeremiah 1:6, NIV). God did reassure this young lad that He would be with him and He would rescue him.

Jeremiah's life played out in a terrible time of war, captivity, and starvation. Jeremiah did answer his call to be a prophet to the nations. He was brave and faithful, and he endured. The message is God uses young people. The apostle Paul told the young Timothy to not let any man despise his youth (1 Timothy 4:12). Young people need to know God has His eye on them and wants to help them and use them and what a great influence they can be with the lost generation of our day.

Today, it's a tough one to get teenagers through the complex-ities of being an adolescent, especially if they're depressed. This section is not a "one and done," as there are a hundred-plus coping skills. Some skills work for this teen, their personality, their life events, as well as current challenges, and some will not as there are many variables. For the parent who wants to try and help their teen find hope, be motivated, and reach their potential, then read on. The information about getting a doctor's evaluation and informing helpful others is the same as advised for helping children. Having a village also pertains.

The CDC reported in 2018–2019 that for teens, depression, substance abuse, and suicide are the most major concerns for twelve- to seventeen-year-olds. Statistics were listed as 15.1 percent of those adolescents had a major depressive episode; 36.7 percent had a persistent feeling of sadness and hopelessness; 18.8 percent seriously considered suicide; 15.7 percent made a serious suicide attempt, and 8.9 percent attempted suicide. Suicide is the second most leading cause of death for teens in the US and Canada.

Highly encourage your teen to tell someone if they are overwhelmed or feel like they would hurt themself. They need the suicide prevention hotline: 800–273–8255. There is also the suicide-preventionlifeline.org and for texting HOME741741.

Skills to try:

1. Try all the skills listed for younger children and modify them for age appropriateness.
2. Talk to your teenager about discovering a new way to look at an old problem.
3. Help them to see how they feel now will pass and they can be happy one day.

4. Advise them on how to stop the self-doubt and to stop underestimating themself. Tell them how important it is to believe in themself and have faith.

5. Assist them in trying visualization, where they use all five senses and go to that happy place in their mind where they feel free, happy, accepted, loved, and not judged.

6. They may need to let go of self-imposed limitations and fear of failure.

7. They could use some self-discovery to make goals toward a life purpose.

8. Guide them to look at their negative life experiences as opportunities where they can find meaning and pay forward to help another.

9. They can journal feelings and include their strengths and what they are grateful for.

10. They need to set boundaries, asking themself if what they are doing is illegal or against their values and goals. They need to ask if what they are involved in will hurt themselves or anyone else. They must examine if their friends are negative or positive and if a change in friends may be necessary.

11. Building resilience is a must for this day and age's young people. See the section addressing this.

12. Expose them to young people who are role models or at least read about role models. One positive example is Simone Biles, the Olympian in Tokyo who had the courage to speak out against abuse and seek help for her mental illness. I applaud her. Role models are not likely to be using drugs, drinking, or smoking.

13. Talk to your teen about courage and why they may be feeling inadequate. Ask them why they are so hard on themself. Ask about their strengths.

14. Teens need to be reminded to treat themselves with the same kindness that they show to others.

15. Steer them away from destructive self-talk. That voice usually carries with it negative buddies such as doubt, fear, blame, and feeling like they should be punished for something. If negative self-talk is persistent or shows up in every area of their life, then seek out a mental health professional. It is often linked with anxiety and depression.

Jeremiah 29:11 (NIV), "'For I know the plans I have for you,' declares the Lord, 'plans to prosper you and not to harm you, plans to give you hope and a future.'"

God is addressing the captive Jews but wants them to not lose hope. God can work through hardships and suffering. We are never forsaken.

Response:

_____

_____

_____

_____

_____

_____

_____

_____

_____

_____

_____

_____

_____

_____

_____

_____

_____

_____

Seniors, Depression, and Peanuts

A bus driver is driving a busload of seniors when he is tapped on the shoulder by a little old lady. She offers him a handful of peanuts, which he gratefully munches on. After about fifteen minutes, she taps him on his shoulder again and gives him another handful of peanuts. She repeats this gesture a few more times. When she is about to hand him another batch, he asks her, "Why don't you eat the peanuts yourself?" She replies, "We can't chew them because we have no teeth." The puzzled driver asks, "Why do you buy them then?" The old lady replies, "We just love to lick the chocolate off of them."

Sometimes the golden years are not so golden. They can be down-right gray (pun intended). Mental Health America reports a statistic that 2 million out of 34 million Americans sixty-five years of age and older suffer from some form of depression. The process of aging has unique challenges, but this page will be on things to try to keep depression at bay. It is a hope you don't just survive but thrive.

The challenges to aging are many, but look on the positive side. Everybody's silver lining will be different than other seniors. Mine is that I own my life now, not work. I have time to write, play with my grandchildren, garden, do other hobbies, volunteer, walk the dog more, exercise, read, travel, pray, counsel, shop, and have lunch with my friends. I am part of a neighborhood ladies' tea. The stage of life you are in is about perspective. That means the way you see and approach life.

I must tell a story about my beloved grandfather William N. Collicutt, who lived to be a hundred. When he was a young man, he lost his daughter to rheumatic fever at age nine, and another daughter became seriously stricken with polio. There was a significant amount of grief, as expected. Much time passed, and Grampa now has us grandchildren. I only knew the loving and delightful Grandpa. He enjoyed things like feeding a stray cat, tending to his rhubarb patch, reading his *Reader's Digest*, and attending church. He welcomed friends and loved it if they would play checkers with him. During summer months in Florida, he fed alligators marshmallows. He kept mentally sharp by these activities, and he stayed able-bodied by mowing the yard until he was ninety-one. Having a purpose was never a problem for him. I loved him so much. I want to be the kind of senior and grandparent so that when I am gone from this world, I will be missed because I loved much. My mother was a very involved grandmother as well. I have learned from two of the best.

If you don't have grandchildren, make sure you have friends. The point is to stay mentally and physically busy as much as your body cooperates. Do fun activities like going with friends on tours of various kinds, such as to a museum or on a bus. Be easy on the driver, though! Read, play games, get a pet (but maybe not an alligator), attend church services of your choosing, or be a part of clubs or volunteer. Be the best influence on the grandchildren.

Seniors who struggle with loneliness do so primarily from missing friends and loved ones who have passed on and from not feeling useful. The latter is something you have to take control over. With Christian work there is always something to do, and with many service organizations, the need for helpers is great. You must find what fits your niche.

John, a disciple of Jesus, preached fearlessly and was a pillar of the church. His influence in his younger and older years was substantial. We have the five books of the Bible he wrote: John, 1, 2, and 3 John, and Revelation. He died in 98 AD as an old man. He was known as the disciple that Jesus loved due to his close personal relationship with the Lord, and he served important roles as the Lord's witness and as a leader in the church. Think about what that actually means for you. In your senior years, you can be significant, which means great, important, or to be worthy of attention. Dig deep for self-discovery.

Skills to try:

1. Do not focus on losses, such as loss of driver's license, youth, health, possessions, finances, home, job, or family and friends. Do not focus on the loss of independence if there is a challenge with doing daily tasks. You can grieve this part of your life, but don't stay there.

2. Accept what you cannot change.

3. Look for your silver lining. Listing them is good. In mine there are more than a dozen.

4. Focus on what you are grateful for.

5. Be part of a community, such as card or garden clubs, game playing, or church.

6. Take up a new hobby. Take up a class. Be creative with exploring art, writing, or music.

7. Exercise. This can even be in a chair if mobility is an issue. Try a new exercise. Make sure it is low impact.

8. Laugh, then laugh some more. Keep your mind strong.

9. Socialize. Do not isolate!

10. Volunteer/give back. It is very fulfilling.

11. Foster or adopt a pet.

12. There are things all around to be explored. Go out and make it an adventure. You will come home probably tired but fulfilled.

13. Take care of your health. It will stimulate your brain and release the feel-good hormones, and you will feel younger.

Isaiah 46:4 (NIV), "Even to your old age and gray hairs I am He, I am He who will sustain you. I have made you and I will carry you: I will sustain you and I will rescue you."

From the cradle to the grave, God sustains us physically, emotionally, mentally, and financially.

Response:

_____

_____

_____

_____

_____

_____

_____

_____

_____

_____

_____

_____

_____

_____

Disappointment

Disappointment in Others

Mario Andretti is considered by many to be the greatest race car driver of all time. He has raced for five decades. He has had one hundred and nine career wins on major circuits and ten crashes. Mario was asked to give advice to other drivers, and he responded, "Don't look at the wall. Your car goes where your eyes go." Your focus then could be staying on the track or going into a wall. This is good life advice. The walls can be considered our obstacles and our wrong focus. The road ahead is where we need to focus.

It is the same for one's emotional health. If you are focused on how other people have disappointed you, then you will stay in that state of apathy, frustration, anger, resentment, and maybe hopelessness. That is sad, actually, because it was likely a case of you having expectations that were too high. There were too many, or they were even out of line with reality. You need to look at where all those expectations came from—you, family, friends, boss, etcetera. Try being a little disappointed in what is very important: what matters to you, then eliminate or cope with what doesn't. Possibly you forgot that people are not mistake-proof. They are just like us, under pressure with things going on at work, home, and school, and they have their own needs and problems. Talk it out with them rather than stay upset.

Where does all that disappointment come from? Did you have childhood trauma or hurtful relationships? Who are you surrounded by—people who manipulate you, misuse you, insult you, disrespect you, or make you feel like you walk on eggshells?

In any case disappointment is sadness involving unfulfilled hopes or expectations. "People avoid disappointment far more than many other emotional experiences. Disappointment comes with finality—the recognition that you don't have, didn't get, or will never achieve whatever it is that you wanted." Sadness from the disappointment will help you remember what it is or was that you desired. It thus gives you a chance to consider revising your objectives and strategies for the future. With disappointment in a relationship, it is easier to protest with anger than encounter your sadness (*Psychology Today*, Mary Lamla, PhD, November 20, 2011).

Here's what not to do. Don't go out with Parry Party to drown out your feelings that life went a different direction than your reality expected. Parry is party hardy, and you may indulge excessively, thinking that drowning out your misery is better. Also, Bessie Been Around is at the party, and that's another sticky-wicky temptation. Don't lose sight of your goals. You may feel like Setback Sal now, but those goals were made when you did not have such jumbled emotions. Get back to clarity of vision and remind yourself that this so-called stumbling block can give you the advantage of learning from it.

Skills to try:

1. You cannot please everyone, and they cannot please you every time. Adjust your thinking and see if your reality is really in reality. Accept mistakes others make as part of life.

2. Write out a list of what is important to you as well as what your goals are, and don't allow yourself to be disappointed with what is important or not on your goal list.

3. Set boundaries. Don't let other people take advantage of you, especially when you are in a chaotic head space. Surround yourself with friends and family who are like Pedro Pick You Up and Camille Compassionate. Perfect Puppy and Kindhearted Kitten are helpful distractions for hugging or as possible pets.

4. Express gratitude. Gratitude and grumbling do not occupy the same space.

5. If disappointment in others is something that is a regular struggle for you, then look at whether or not you have faulty thinking (your thoughts don't line up with reality, and you got used to those errors in thinking). For example: if you don't get invited out with a friend, you think that person hates you when it is a case of them having another priority.

6. Communicate. Listen more effectively to what others are saying. Much of the stress with others comes from not understanding what others are saying. Ask for clarification if necessary.

Ephesians 4:32 (NIV), "Be kind and compassionate to one another, forgiving each other, just as in Christ God forgave you."

This is how to relate to others, which includes those who disappoint us. Don't you love being around people who are gracious to you when you have shortcomings?

Response:

_____

_____

_____

_____

_____

_____

_____

_____

_____

_____

_____

_____

_____

_____

_____

_____

_____

_____

The Magnifying Glass Is Not Needed

"Most things disappoint 'til you look deeper" (Graham Greene).

"Disappointment is just a term for our refusal to look on the bright side" (Richelle E. Goodrich).

A magnifying glass is to make objects appear much larger. Disappointment will wear you out, emotionally and physically. We have put a magnifying glass on the wrong things. We live, so we will be disappointed. We are flawed people, and we live in a fallen world. What could go wrong? Well, anything and almost everything. The problem is our focus is misguided. There is the focus on feeling overworked and unappreciated at work and the focus on achieving goals, but maybe not all of them get met. Therefore, one is left feeling like life is just another day of unhappiness.

There is the spotlight on external factors, such as the things you thought would make you happy but didn't; a promotion you received, but it caused more work; a child that is making different career choices than what you thought was best; and a spouse that you have lost the spark with. Your dream home or vehicle you waited years to get needs expensive repairs. You may have been disappointed because a promise that was made to you personally was treated lightly, and your feelings were trampled on. That may have hurt the friendship. Imagine how an Olympian must have felt coming in fourth after many years of training. There is no metal or accolades. There are hundreds of things to be disappointed with.

The outlook should be on the things that empower you. You must realize ruminating over your quagmire will keep you in a pit. You cannot be forward-thinking when it is full of "Oh, no, that will never work out" or "What were you thinking?" Take charge of your life. Make goals and an action plan. Know your strengths and weaknesses. If self-esteem took a nosedive due to not getting the job, then have a plan for what's next. If you had a breakup, then mourn and talk about it, but keep it constructive and see if you learned something important. Surround yourself with positive people.

I recall an interview I did with the school board in which I was asked about my computer skills. I said what I knew and what I didn't know, as I thought I should be honest. I did not get that job. I did get a better job with good benefits, and I stayed there for fifteen years. I was also disappointed in a vacation where I had planned on daily hiking, but my dog had no such plans and resisted adamantly. Really, my dog, who loves walking, decided that the smells of bears, deer, and other creatures in mother nature were not good for her insecurity. I decided to go in the opposite direction and hit the bakery. Well, at least my taste buds were soothed. No judging, please!

Disappointment could be a major concern if it stays with us all day and affects our every day, then our tomorrow, and into the next year. May it not be so! Turn your attention on the Lord, who has the ability to turn your loss, sadness, and letdowns into something good. He knows our situation, and He has the answers. He had the answers before we had the problem. He does not ever say, "Oh, what a fine fix Pat has gotten herself in; well, good luck." The Lord loves it when you give Him all the things that you feel disenchanted about; allow Him to intervene, take control of, and change an outcome in your favor. Please ask the Lord to get involved, to interrupt the woes of the situation, and to bring His perfect results. The Lord knows how to pull off a miracle. If He is in the game of your life, He knows how to do a "shutout play" so the negative will not be so negative and that marvelous favor of His blessings will manifest.

Skills to try:

1. Look for what others intended in a situation that disappointed you, not your feelings, which could be skewed. Don't take it personally.

2. Move forward. Let go of the things in which you are beating yourself up or limiting yourself.

3. Hope gets one through a grievous situation. It also builds resilience. Hope lessens fear, anxiety, and self-doubt. Hope causes one to have confidence that they can get through their plight. It will make you feel like you have some control. Hope does not allow pessimistic thoughts to take control. Hope focuses on the positive. Look for something to be grateful for. Keep hope.

4. Do not keep any anger toward God for allowing a circumstance to happen. You can tell Him how you feel, but don't allow any distance to grow between you and God. The Lord already knows you have disappointment, fear, anger, or frustration. By allowing us to experience struggles, our faith grows. Pray and praise Him and look for His outcome. It will be good.

Ecclesiastes 3:11 (NIV), "He has made everything beautiful in its time."

God is behind the way things are and the way they will be. Things that happen do so when they should, as He has a plan, even if it does not make sense to us. With God there is no happenstance, which means with God there is no coincidence. We have plans for how we think things should work out, but we often forget God has His timing, and it is perfect. Let's go with the perfect plan from the Sovereign God. It will take patience and trust, but it will be worth it.

Response:

_____

_____

_____

_____

_____

_____

_____

_____

_____

_____

_____

_____

_____

_____

_____

_____

_____

_____

_____

_____

_____

_____

Let Go and Hold On

Huh? What do you mean let go and hold on? That sounds like an oxymoron. It means you let go of your disappointments and you hold on to your dreams. You hold on to hope.

This story is about two brothers, Bert and John Jacobs. The year is 1989, and these two bros had a dream to sell tee shirts. They wanted the message on those tee shirts to be one of optimism, simplicity, humor, and humility. But after five years of pounding the streets, living in a van, and eating peanut butter and jelly sandwiches, they still were disappointed that the tee shirts were barely selling. By 1994 they became quite desperate to keep their dream alive. Returning home to Boston, inspiration came as John drew a happy person with a big smile. With less than one hundred dollars left, they put that grin on tee shirts, and they sold out what inventory they had. The boys are now listed as having made millions just by holding onto their dreams and having an optimistic message, ingenuity, and hard work. The tee shirt brand is Life Is Good.

You might think, *That's nice*, but you are still reeling from your own disappointments. That's where the first part of the equation comes in—to give up what is holding you bound, downed, frowned, and on the ground. The second part is to hold on to what could be, such as a dream. Never ever let go of hope. *Oxford Dictionary* states hope is a feeling of expectation and desire for a certain thing to happen. It is an optimistic state of mind based on the expectation of a positive outcome.

Hope reminds me of this little saying, "I want to be like a sunflower so that even on the darkest days, I will stand tall and find the sunlight (Sonlight)."

Hope keeps you going. When disappointment seems to have locked you out, hope helps you find another way in. Hope will remind you, "Don't give up." It calls attention to the fact that there is a bigger picture. Hope lies with us believers that the Lord's presence is with us to give us wisdom and comfort in the hard part of these challenges. His special kind of peace is like none other for the dark emotional moments. Well, it is there for us all of the day and night, but I think especially when we feel broken.

You may have disappointment in yourself, disappointment in other people, or disappointment in something. For example, I was disappointed in myself when I was graduating with my master's degree and missed the honor roll by a tenth of a point. I have been disappointed many times with other people due to their poor decisions mostly, but I had to realize it was not in my control. There were things or objects that disappointed me, such as the car breaking down at a very inconvenient time and vacation not going well.

The problem is we set ourselves up for disappointment to get worse and turn to depression if we expect we can't be happy if we don't get what we expected. You set yourself up for disappointment if you could not control the outcome but thought you could. Disappointment will happen if you want certainty and perfection and you forget the future is fickle. Disappointment's cousins are Randy Regret and Frances Frustration. They may want to visit you and stay awhile. They may even pick up Alice Angry as they travel down the road on the way to your house. This trio would not be uplifting. Unwillingness to accept the reality that you did not get what was expected is what can trigger anger.

Don't wallow in your loss, heartache, or disappointment, as it will make you feel stuck. Letdowns are temporary even if it does not feel like it. It may have felt as if life bullied you like you were up against the giant Goliath. Be sure you are not judging yourself too harshly and not blaming others. In the Bible story about the underdog, David was up against Goliath; Goliath went down. Tell that to yourself very reflectively—Goliath went down.

Skills to try:

1. Decide what is causing your disappointment and do something to make yourself feel better. Keep your routine and keep making plans for your future.

2. Correct any wrong assumptions so you will be smarter and learn from them.

3. Ask yourself if your expectations are unreasonable, unrealistic, inflexible, or selfish.

4. Are you clear on your communication so people understand what is expected?

5. Redirect your sad energy and focus on positive solutions.

6. Could your disappointment just be a problem that needs to be solved?

7. It's okay to grieve a loss, but don't stay there too long, and don't rehearse your misery.

Psalm 42:11 (NIV), "Why so downcast, oh my soul? Why so disturbed within me? Put your hope in God, for I will praise Him, my savior and my God."

You can never go wrong with keeping hope and praising God.

Response:

_____

_____

_____

_____

_____

_____

_____

_____

_____

_____

_____

_____

_____

_____

_____

_____

_____

_____

_____

_____

It Is Worse than Disappointment

A lady's dishwasher stopped working, so she called a repairman. He was not able to accommodate an evening appointment, so she informed him where she would leave the key for the next day and her check for the service. She advised the man that he did not need to worry about her Rottweiler, Brutus. However, she strongly warned the man not to talk to her parrot. The repair man went into the home and noticed the Rottweiler was the biggest, meanest-looking dog he had ever seen. True to the homeowner's report, he just lay there watching the man do the repair. The parrot, on the other hand, incessantly squawked, getting on the man's last nerve. Finally, he had enough and told the parrot off, to which the parrot replied, "Get him, Brutus."

The parrot in the story is smart, and it is a cute story/joke, but know that parrots are similar to us humans in that they can get discouraged. Some of those reasons are: they live to about eighty years old and could have an owner change and get passed on to someone who may keep them in a cage out of the way and not interact with them. They experience discouragement and loneliness if they lose a mate. They may have a dirty cage or be ill or injured, or the parrot might be bored.

To live is to have disappointment. But discouragement is a bit worse. It is being deprived of courage and confidence. One feels despair, defeat, dejection, hopelessness, and disheartened. Enthusiasm is almost depleted.

What causes someone to go from disappointment to discouragement? Possibly life has really weighed you down; you are overly tired and overwhelmed, and circumstances have made you cry more than usual. Stress may be heavy. A person with an overly sensitive soul can be more prone to discouragement. Someone can also be feeling like a failure, or the situation they face seems to not let up. Frustration, worry, and anxiety seem to be sticking to you like glue. The discouraged person may feel like their life is out of control. Your fight and your faith may have taken a back seat.

Negative self-talk is a big precursor for discouragement. That spiel of negatives you think in your head all day will keep you down like a leaded balloon. You think that is not you, but catch yourself with things like "I don't feel like going there," or "I don't play golf very well; you find someone else," or "I think I will just eat this bucket of fried chicken and chocolate cake."

The opposite of discouragement is courage. Courage is not all about doing something that you find fearful but about having the strength to persevere and withstand in the midst of something painful, damaging, negative, or full of grief. Courage is needed so you don't give up but continue to reach for what is important to you.

Jonah is a Bible character (Jonah 1:15–17) who was thrown overboard, then swallowed by a great fish. But God must have talked to the great fish and told the fish, "Don't chew." He commanded the fish to vomit Jonah up onto dry land after three days. A sperm whale is the only whale that has a throat big enough to swallow a human. If it was a whale—we don't know for sure—then Jonah got by the whale's teeth and was in the stomach part, which had a bunch of digestive acids. Wouldn't that be discouragement and fright beyond measure? When you feel like you could be "chewed up" by the teeth of life or even left lonely, bored, and uncared for like the parrot, then always hold onto the fact that God talked to a big fish and got Jonah out of a very nasty situation and he survived with no bite marks on his body. It is a miracle and an amazing one.

Skills to try:

1. It is okay to acknowledge you are discouraged. Ask for some support.
2. Let go of what is negative, like anger, regret, or even toxic relationships.
3. Don't try to control things beyond your control.
4. Focus on what you do best.
5. Find a friend and be a friend.
6. Write a list of ways you can encourage yourself. Put those in your day.
7. Reward yourself for achievements. Maybe try something new.
8. Help somebody else.
9. List ways you will reduce your stress, then do those things. Put fun in your life.
10. Express gratitude regularly.
11. Be careful you are not full of complaints. It's really a bad attitude.

Psalm 34:19-20 (NIV), "A righteous man may have many troubles, but the Lord delivers him from them all, He protects all his bones, not one of them will be broken."

It may not be a life that is carefree, but the Lord promises to intervene. He will come through with what we need.

Response:

_____

_____

_____

_____

_____

_____

_____

_____

_____

_____

_____

_____

_____

_____

_____

_____

_____

_____

_____

_____

_____

_____

Worry

Worry Makes Me Feel Beat Up

You may think this title is harsh, but worry is harsh. It will run you over, drive away, then come back and run over you again, and it can do that a hundred and sixty-eight hours in a week. Any sleep you might get will be fretful. Don't forget the snowball effect—it gets bigger as it goes down your mountain. It is also a huge waste of time to entertain.

Do not entertain any members of the Worry family in your home, especially Brother Sam Stone Broke Worry, Sister Paula Poor Health Worry, Uncle Walter Wrecked Relationship Worry, and Charlie Challenging Kids Worry. These are fictitious to make a point that if you see yourself falling into worry, say, "No, I will not be like Olivia Overwhelmed Worry."

Before you think that is not you: worry over finances, health, relationships, and the kids—ask yourself if you are a master over it. If not, stay tuned; hope is available also a hundred and sixty-eight hours a week. It is in the promises of God and the indwelling Christ. Think of it this way: the One who is the complete victor resides in us if we invite Him into our heart.

If things do not feel good in any way, perhaps this example of David will give some insight. In Psalm 55 David goes from his personal anguish and complaints to a confession of how he will handle his life in verse 23 (NIV), "As for me, I trust in you." David experienced the bear, the lion, the Philistine giant, and someone in authority who wanted to eliminate him. David teaches a good skill—put things in God's hand. Do not doubt that God will come through. It might not look like it or feel like it, but God's very nature is to come through even when it looks hopeless. Do your part to trust and develop skills to cope while you keep hope alive.

Ask yourself, "Will anything change if I worry about it?" And ask, "What are the things I can control?" How have you successfully dealt with worry in the past? Who or what do you need to take the first step to gain control over worry? No matter how difficult things are, remind yourself that you have the power within yourself to be an overcomer. Consider this—does worry help you pay the bills, fix the broken car, or get Wayward Warren back on track? Does worry help you deal with Boss Lady Beatrice? I expect you said no. Well, worry tends to give you a lot of mental tension, then physical tension. That in itself will make one feel like they need to worry.

These words in your head—always, nobody, everybody, should, shouldn't, have to, nothing, never, and can't—are a tip that you are worrying. Talk back to them. You can also picture the word or worry expression in a balloon and pop it, saying, "Not happening, Waldo Worry; get away." Then replace it with nonchalant words that calm you. Don't say, "I will never finish that project"; say, "I will give it my best." Don't say, "I will get fired for being late"; say, "I will be okay; if I need to, I will tell the boss about the accident that held me up."

Skills to try:

1. Consider this—give all your worries to the Lord, and He, in turn, gives His protection, stability, peace, and joy. It is a trust thing. It is also a great trade.

2. Tell yourself you are in charge of your emotions, not worry being large and in charge. Be Master Mark or Victorious Vicky.

3. Do not succumb to the thoughts you know will enslave you. Hopefully you have Christ as the grandmaster. It will take some practice to undo years of worry.

Psalm 55:22 (NIV), "Cast your cares on the Lord and He will sustain you: He will never let the righteous fall."

Focus on these words: you cast; He sustains, and He never will let you fall. It is a promise.

Response:

_____

_____

_____

_____

_____

_____

_____

_____

_____

_____

_____

_____

_____

_____

_____

_____

_____

_____

_____

_____

Five Pounds of Worry

I am unapologetically a dog lover. I could not help myself from using a Chihuahua for this example of worry. Why? Because this wonderful little animal can be shaky and stressed out, usually for no reason unless the dog is cold. The chihuahua is tiny, but worry can be big. The little dog can rule your house just like worry tries to rule you. Their personality is larger than life, and worry will be large and in charge if you let it. This petit dog may bark a lot, and if you ask me, worry "barks" a lot in your head with a noise that you will wish you could turn off, especially at night when you want to sleep. These little dogs can be prone to some health issues such as epilepsy, mitral value concern, and kneecaps that pop out of place. Chronic worry can cause you to have health issues such as suppression of your immune system, digestive disorders, muscle tension, artery disease, and short-term memory loss.

Can you relate to being worried about nothing like this dog? Worry is a focus on what might happen in the future or is currently happening, but the mind dwells on the difficulty. It leaves one feeling stressed, anxious, uneasy, fatigued, alarmed, apprehensive, frustrated, irritated, and even tormented. Yes, tormented in serious cases, as it can leave the person in anguish of body and mind. Ongoing worry can quickly turn into chronic stress, which will affect one's ability to do their activities of daily living. It can give you a bad case of insomnia. If you can't get rid of that migraine, see if you are in worry mode.

The difference between worry, stress, and anxiety is worry is temporary, and anxiety can be chronic and debilitating. Stress is a response to life's challenges, pressures, and threats and usually goes away when the stressor leaves. Negative thoughts about stress are worries. Worry tends to be repetitive and even obsessive.

Worry is a bully. You have to fight back. You cannot dwell in the "what-ifs" of life. It is a lovely feeling to feel secure and have nothing to be concerned with, but life happens fast, leaving us with a feeling we can't control; thus, we worry. I personally like my ducks all in a row, but when it does not happen, I do my best to choose the opposite of worry, and that is trust. That is actually a great trade. I give my worry to the Lord, and He gives me peace of mind and heart.

"Worry implies that we don't quite trust that God is big enough, powerful enough, or loving enough to take care of what happens in our life" (Francis Chan).

Skills to try:

1. Make peace with the idea that life may not go as planned or even well. It's life; it happens.
2. Do not focus on things out of your control. Some things will just be out of control.
3. Can you turn what you are worried about into action and problem-solving?
4. Face what you are worrying about. Are you procrastinating or delaying making a decision?
5. If you are like me and you want all your ducks in a row, it means you want to organize and be well-prepared for your day/tasks. However, when life goes haywire and that does not happen, can you get the mentality of going with the flow? Try just being present and not letting yourself get distracted.

Psalm 16:8 (NIV), "I have set the Lord always before me. Because He is at my right hand I will not be shaken."

This has security all over it. The Lord is at our side, so we should not be unsettled.

Response:

_____

_____

_____

_____

_____

_____

_____

_____

_____

_____

_____

_____

_____

_____

_____

_____

_____

_____

_____

_____

It Could Be Worry, or It Could Be Concern

A man went out to dinner and worried that his potato was bad. He called the waitress over and explained his concern. She nodded, picked up his potato, and smacked it. Then she put it back on his plate and said, "If that potato causes you any more concern, you just let me know."

With all the talk about not worrying as the Word of God tells us not to, it can make a person wonder if they are in worry mode or concerned mode. The difference between worry and concern is worry controls you, and concern shows interest and regard. They are close in meaning, but worry suggests fretting, which can involve anxiety and restlessness. Concern usually will lead one to do something like pray, take a meal to someone, give money, give a person a ride, or watch someone's child or pet. Worry expects things to go wrong, and concern deals with facts and problem-solving. Worry can be incessant and destructive, as it leads to stress. Concern prepares you for life's challenges and a desire to solve the problem or minimize it. It is a positive action.

Worrying means you took it upon yourself to handle it. In essence it is like saying, "God, I can do a better job." Worry also means you took it too far and thus came out from under the protection of God's goodness, grace, help, mercy, wisdom, and power.

Let me clarify: We will always have concerns. After all, there is a pandemic to be concerned about. There are others that tell us about their problems. There are bills that pile up and parents who are aging. There is the daughter dating Bad Boy Billy and the son who is hanging out with Carl Cocaine. There is the toddler who has more energy than an athlete. The forty-hour work week; oh, say no more.

When you worry so much, you get stuck in the "what-ifs" of life. For example, mine was back years ago when it was my turn to host church group at our house. My thinking was, *What if the dog barks, the phone rings, or the baby cries at an inopportune time?* I should have been thinking that these guests knew I have a dog, a baby, and a phone, and that is just life. If that happens, I can excuse myself and get up and take care of it. Well, I made a mountain out of a molehill. I caused myself undue stress. In hindsight, the baby can be soothed, and I can leave the room; the phone can be unplugged, and the dog can be put out. The problem is worriers are not so good at problem-solving. They are into thinking that bad things will happen in the future.

Wade Worry needed a break from his distress, so he took a road trip with the cousins Amelia Anxiety and Felix Fear. Along the way they picked up a couple of classmates named Igor Impatience and Francine Frustration. Igor was full of fool-hardy decisions, and Francine was showing her temper. If only they could all learn some coping skills. Oh wait, the skills are in this book.

Remember the childhood story of Jack and the Beanstalk? Jack planted some magic bean seeds, and they turned into a giant beanstalk. At the top was an angry giant. Stretch with me to make a point. Worry is like Jack's beanstalk. It grew astonishingly big, and at the top of it was a "giant" problem. Worries actually grow fast and multiply. Jack knew what to do to stop the worry—he chopped down the beanstalk, and that was the end of the giant. You have the power to stop worrying.

Skills to try:

1. Don't shut God out of your issues. Isn't God able to do the impossible? Practice thanking God for His divine care and consult Him for His solutions. Now you have hope instead of hopelessness. You have a lighter load instead of a futile heavy load.

2. Learn some problem-solving. I put it like this: First clarify what you need to solve, decide all the possibilities, and choose one that works. Consult trusted family and friends for ideas if needed.

3. To chop down your beanstalk of worry, you should try channeling your negative thinking and your overthinking into something else. You can release that energy into doing something physical. Overthinking is marked by excessive worry about things out of your control. When my mind is racing faster than an antelope can run and I want to sleep, I must get out of bed, meditate or pray and do something relaxing. Don't turn on any screens, as they produce blue light, which causes problems with the brain turning off to sleep.

Second Corinthians 11:28 (NIV), "Besides everything else, I face daily the pressure of my concern for all the churches."

Caring for a church and others can be a burden but an act of love. Paul was concerned, not worried.

Response:

_____

_____

_____

_____

_____

_____

_____

_____

_____

_____

_____

_____

_____

_____

_____

_____

_____

_____

_____

_____

_____

To Help Stop Worry—Read

This title means, "Read these quotes that will hopefully inspire you." Of course, it will not totally stop worry, as there is work to do to stop this habit or even this obsession. But quotes give one food for thought and may trigger a new way of looking at your situation. It may be so catchy or encouraging that you will memorize it and use it when worry knocks at your door or use it to help others. After all, helping others is a mood booster.

"That the birds of worry and care fly over your head, this you cannot change, but that they build nests in your hair, this you can prevent" (Chinese proverb).

"Stop being afraid of what could go wrong, and start being excited of what could go right" (Tony Robbins).

"Worry is like a rocking chair, it gives you something to do but gets you nowhere" (Erma Bombeck).

"Worry is worshiping the problem" (Toby Mac).

"Worry is thinking that has turned toxic" (Harold B. Walker).

George F. Burns was asked what the most important key to longevity was, and he reported, "It was to avoid, worry, stress and tension." (He lived to be a hundred years old.)

"I have held many things in my hand and I have lost them all, but whatever I have placed in God's hand, that I still possess" (Corrie ten Boom, Holocaust concentration camp survivor).

"There isn't enough room in your mind for both worry and faith. You must decide which one will live there" (marcandangel. com).

This delightful story also has a message. It is paraphrased, and the author is unknown.

A man was on a long flight when an announcement came on to fasten the seatbelts, as turbulence was ahead. Passengers began to look apprehensive as the approaching storm suddenly broke. There were cracks of thunder and lightning dancing across the dark sky. The man looked around the plane and saw nearly all the passengers were fearful except one little girl. The plane lurched this way and that, but the little girl remained calm. When the plane safely landed, the man went and asked the child, "How did you manage to not be afraid?" She replied, "'Cause my daddy's the pilot, and he's taking me home."

So our Father is the pilot, and He is in control, and He will bring us safely home. So forget the host of things to worry about.

Skills to try:

1. Go to your prayer place and give God all your fears and worries and take His protection, stability, place of refuge, and fullness of joy.

2. Write down the negative things about worry and see if you get an idea for your own positive quote to live by.

3. Worry is about the past and what might happen in the future. Try asking yourself, "What do I smell, see, hear, feel, and taste?" Try and replace your worry habit with an "exploration of your senses" habit to do daily. This is essentially a pause and a distraction to take you away from the stress.

4. When your head hits the pillow at night and worry takes over your sweet dream time, tell worry "no" and replace it with a favorite relaxing song.

John 14:27 (NIV), "Peace I leave with you; my peace I give

you; not as the world gives. Do not let your hearts be troubled and do not be afraid."

In the midst of troubles, there is a peace of mind and heart that comes to those who are yielded to Jesus.

Response:

_____

_____

_____

_____

_____

_____

_____

_____

_____

_____

_____

_____

_____

_____

_____

Fear

You Can Conquer Fear

"Don't be pushed around by the fears in your mind, be led by the dreams in your heart" (Roy T. Bennett).

I am talking about fear. You are probably thinking you can't conquer it. Could it have been with you a long time? Would it add too much unwanted stress with your anxiety already high? Are you thinking the fear is too big to take it on? No, that would be telling yourself you feel helpless. You are not helpless. However, you don't like how you feel. You might feel like it is a hill of manure in front of you that you can't get over. I use that analogy, as my sister and I had to run from a bull when we were very young, and we ran up a manure hill. But my instincts were to do it so we wouldn't have gotten possibly gored. We were making a shortcut and should have known better. That "should have known better" means we all make a mistake.

Fear and uncertainty are strong emotions that will hold you on a manure hill. Fear is a natural response to things we don't understand that threaten our safety or health. A bull chasing me was indeed a threat to my safety. The adrenal glands released adrenaline into my bloodstream, so away I went to escape/survive. It's the fight-or-flight mode. It's a wonderful way God made us.

Don't let fear call the shots. You are in charge. If fear takes over your life, it will get stronger. You will feel less competent and think a bit less of yourself, as you won't feel like you can overcome it. Fear will cause a host of physical problems, such as having a weakened immune system, ulcers, cardiovascular problems, irritable bowel, and premature aging, and those are just a few. So a person can keep the fear and have frequent infections, a perforation, a potential heart attack, pain, diarrhea, or an inflamed bowel and look older quicker, or one can learn some skills and put fear in its place.

The characteristics of fearless people are: they readily acknowledge their fears but don't let them overtake them, and they are not easily swayed by emotions. They are realistic, unconventional, and proud of it; they know when to relish control, are self-confident, maintain awareness of their surroundings, and are grateful and willing to share. Fearless people try and balance all aspects of their life. They are prepared for the worst-case scenario, and they have a backup plan for that plan. Fear does not stop them, but the opposite happens; it causes them to spring into action. This one is important—fearless people do not listen to their inner critic. They may fall down, but they will "claw their way back up." They don't stop learning and reading. Fearless people can readily laugh at themselves. Valiant people have valiant role models and are not afraid to ask for help (Hack Spirit, September 25, 2021).

What are some of those things on your manure pile? Does it include fear of failure, fear of what others would think, fear of being replaced or not being loved, fear of being poor, getting older, and dying? Is there a fear of being criticized, making mistakes, or making commitments? Is there a fear of change, being alone, or feeling inadequate? Do you fear being vulnerable?

Skills to try:

1. The fourth paragraph describes the characteristics of a fearless person. Which ones do you want to work on? Get a game plan in place to do that. I can believe that if you told some trusted people that you had some things you wanted to work on, they would be glad to help you.

2. Analyze what your fears are. Be empowered. You will need to take the dread out of your situation. An example is to build a skill such as public speaking. Take charge.

3. Work on those things that are on your personal fear list (your manure pile). Work on only the ones that are important to you right now. For instance, I am not going to try and conquer my fear of bungee jumping, as it is not important to me.

4. When fear has caused great physical discomfort, emotional anguish, and mental turmoil, it could be time to seek professional help.

Jeremiah 17:7 (NIV), "Blessed is the man who trusts in the Lord, whose confidence is in Him."

In its simplicity, we will be blessed if we trust the Lord. That includes trusting Him with the feared things.

Response:

_____

_____

_____

_____

_____

_____

_____

_____

_____

_____

_____

_____

_____

_____

_____

_____

_____

_____

_____

The Yo-Yo of Fear

Fear is a complex emotion caused by impending danger, a state of alarm, or dread for the safety of oneself or others. It is a natural condition we all experience that can be safe and positive, or it can have negative consequences.

When you recognize a fear, your amygdala in the brain alerts your nervous system, which sets stress hormones (cortisol and adrenaline) to work. The body then decides whether to fight, flight, or freeze. It is a warning to survive. When experiencing fear, the brain may reroute energy to the amygdala, where there would be a slowing down of processing in other areas. At this point it may be difficult to speak or make a rational decision. The fight response means confronting the threat aggressively, and the flight means running from the danger. These responses are automatic.

Fear and anxiety seem to be attached at the hip. Frequent intense fear responses where there is not an actual threat are anxiety. Think what that does to the body. Activate and deactivate the responses—your body will feel constant anxiety, and you will feel like a yo-yo. Depending on the person, it might take twenty to thirty minutes to recover from one scary event, and then away the response goes again. Your nervous system is quite thrown off, and those automatic functions can stop working properly. A yo-yo toy goes up and down on a string and spins around. If you don't get your fear responses/anxiety under control, you will feel like a yo-yo. A suggestion is when you are trying to regain your composure after a threat, perceived or real, to find a calm place and do deep breathing.

The year my son was in Afghanistan as a marine, I had a fear that the marine corps vehicle would pull up with someone who would give me the news that he was injured severely or he died. I had a bad case of insomnia for many months. Before you think I should have been able to spiritually handle anything as I was mature in my walk with the Lord, allow me to say emotions came into play and remember there is a biochemical response going on as well. What really helped me manage the fear was to get a scripture I could hold onto and claim in prayer. Mine was Isaiah 43:5 (NIV), "Do not be afraid, for I am with you; I will bring your children from the East." I prayed that for his whole platoon. Also, I prayed he would be able to do Psalm 18:29 (NIV), "With your help I can advance against a troop; with my God I can scale a wall." This last one may be helpful to you—Psalm 138:7 (NIV), "Though I walk in the midst of trouble, you preserve my life." You can have a "loss" frame of thinking, which is hard to overcome without divine intervention to help that fearful thinking. Garden therapy and giving praise to God were some of my other coping skills.

The Bible records a story in Numbers 13 and 14 about spies/ leaders who were sent out to explore the land of Canaan. Twelve came back, and ten of them reported the inhabitants were powerful and of great size. They reported they seemed like grasshoppers compared to them. Fear gripped the ten, causing a ripple effect, and the other campers became full of terror. The people were on the edge of entering the promised land, but instead they rebelled and lost faith. See what fear does? It will cause you to feel vexed, hexed, and perplexed.

Skills to try:

1. Learn to distinguish between real and perceived threats. You will need to discern between those that could actually bring harm and those that feel real and bring you needless anxiety.

156

2. Don't make things bigger than they are. Focus on what you need to do next.

3. Have a game plan in place if you know there could be a potentially fearful situation. For example: hiking in the mountains where black bears, cougars, and pit vipers live. I also have a loud whistle.

4. Get scriptures that pertain to your circumstance; pray that word, and trust God.

Isaiah 41:10 (NIV), "So, do not fear, for I am with you; do not be dismayed, for I am your God. I will strengthen you and help you; I will uphold you with my righteous right hand."

God will be with us always. We are not to be dismayed, especially at unexpected things, as He offers His perfect strength and help. Upholding is standing up for us and supporting us.

Response:

_____

_____

_____

_____

_____

_____

_____

_____

_____

_____

_____

_____

_____

_____

_____

_____

_____

_____

_____

_____

_____

Doctor Octopus

Doctor Octopus was Spider-Man's archenemy in the movie *Spider-Man 2* in 2004. You need to look at fear as your enemy. Why? It's because it can paralyze you with fear. It is like Doctor Octopus in that it can be cruel and brutal to you. Doctor Octopus had four extra "tentacles" that resembled an octopus' tentacles. A real octopus has eight tentacles. Here are the eight tentacles of fear that could be detrimental to you if you allow them to:

1. Fear can rob you of peace and joy. That is due to being consumed with it and feeling overwhelmed. Fear disconnects us from all the fullness God has in store for us.

2. Fear can cause long-term mental health effects, such as fatigue, clinical depression, anxiety, and post-traumatic stress.

3. Fear can weaken your immune system, cause cardiovascular damage and gastrointestinal problems, and age you prematurely.

4. Fear can cause social issues. Groups of people may fear for their safety on a regular basis because of their skin color, their sexual identification, or gender.

5. Fear can cause people to not leave home. They feel anguish if they do. Home feels like the only safe place.

6. Fear can open the door to other negative spirits. It gives the devil power to operate in your life.

7. Fear can control you. It keeps you in a cycle of defeat. It controls what you think, feel, and do.

8. Fear can cause you to get stuck where you can't eat, sleep, concentrate, work, or enjoy life.

It is important to identify what your fears are. Pinpoint them and face them, or they can control you. Taking action will help you break the "hold of suction of the tentacles." Courage and then confidence seem to develop when you confront your fears. You will feel like you were able to exert power so you could be in charge of your life, not fear being in charge. It will also help develop resilience, and you will feel stronger to manage future fears.

Have you experienced how you may feel more understanding of other people who may have had the same fear (flying, anesthesia, snakes, public speaking, or driving on an eight-lane highway)? By the way, the eight-lane highway going around San Diego was my aversion, and I chose to face it. I made several angst noises that expressed my trepidation, but when the ride was complete, I felt good about myself. I even had my passenger take a picture in case my family, who might have been doubters, could see I did it.

Babe Ruth, who played twenty-two seasons of baseball, gave this valuable quote, "Never let the fear of striking out keep you from playing the game."

Skills to try:

1. When fear comes to grab you with its powerful suckers, you need to peel the suckers away from you (figuratively). Start looking at the evidence. Challenge the fearful thought. For example, if you fear a recluse spider, ask yourself if you have ever encountered a recluse spider. (A recluse spider is shy and avoids humans; its bite is very rare). What would you tell a friend who was scared of it?

2. Take slow and deep breaths. This will decrease the release of the stress hormone cortisol and help you relax. It will also lower your heart rate and regulate your blood pressure.

3. Say positive affirmations, such as "I am going to overcome this" and "I am capable of being at rest and peace." In fact, a good skill is to tell yourself three positive affirmations every day.

Second Timothy 1:7 (NIV), "God did not give us a spirit of fear, but a spirit of power, love, and a sound mind."

There you have it. God gave it to us and the three together: power, love, and a sound mind are the antidote for fear. Fear could very well be the opposite of faith.

Response:

_____

_____

_____

_____

_____

_____

_____

_____

_____

_____

_____

_____

_____

_____

_____

_____

A Challenging Condition and Fearful Family

Nobody wants it, that anxious feeling, but it's an inevitable part of life. Anxiety is also normal and reasonable with certain everyday challenges, such as loss, an illness, an exam one needs to pass, financial challenges, an interview, or relationship disagreements. Anxiety seems to have worry attached to it. That attached worry could be out of proportion to the likelihood of the feared thing ever happening. Examine if it is. Anxiety can be worse for the person who had a negative childhood.

Fear is a dreadful family member to anxiety as well. There is Uncle Frank Failure Fear, Aunt Rachel Rejection Fear, Grandma Irene Illness Fear, Brother Carl Can't Cope Fear, Sister Lorie Lose Control Fear, Grandpa Larry Lonely Fear, Cousin Carly Catastrophe Fear, and Niece Fran Future Fear. Do you see yourself in any of these? Do you fear you will fail, be rejected, be ill, not be able to cope, lose control, be lonely, have a catastrophe, or fear anything about the future?

Spending time with Mother Earth can help relieve stress and anxiety, improve your mood, and boost feelings of happiness. Whatever you call it—forest bathing, ecotherapy, meditation/ prayer in nature, green time, or the wilderness cure—your brain will benefit from time in nature. Here is a natural cure from the American Heart Association (paraphrased).

1. If depressed: Get out to green, natural spaces. Try a stroll in the forest, hills, or meadows.
2. If stressed: Nature has a way of calming your nerves due to its beauty and the sounds that soothe you. Just looking at nature causes the mind to shift away from the stressors and observe and feel what relaxes you.

3. If anxious: Working out in nature helps to reduce anxiety even more than going to a gym. Get the best mental bang for your buck by hitting some trails.

4. If self-involved: If you are having trouble with dwelling on what is wrong in your life, then getting in nature shifts the focus off of yourself onto things of interest. Research shows that walking in nature for ninety minutes versus being in an urban area for the same amount of time helps the part of the brain that is linked to negative rumination.

5. If fatigued: The brain gets tired from multitasking. Your prefrontal cortex will need a time-out to recharge from the brain overload. Time in nature will help your brain rest, be restored, and be more able to refocus. Being in nature energizes.

6. If uninspired: If you change the scenery from a screen to nature, it can't help but inspire creativity. The change can lead to natural inspiration, innovation, fascination, and contentment.

7. If antisocial: Time in the natural world can help with your personal relationships. Natural beauty results in more prosocial behaviors, like generosity and empathy.

8. If disconnected: Nature makes one feel like they belong to an expansive world. This is vital to well-being. Being outside makes you feel more alive and can help you keep a wider perspective, which may help you have an improved mood and connection with others.

9. If angsty: If you feel lost and wonder what life is all about, then a dose of awe might remind you how wonderous the world is. Look at the trees that are hundreds of years old, the mountains that seem to touch the clouds, and a sky full of uncountable stars.

There is always hope, even though it might feel quite futile. Little by little, you can take control back. Having faith is restful, but fear is stressful. Keep the faith. Check your "cannot thinking," such as "I cannot get up and take care of myself" or "I cannot get a better job." Add to that "I cannot make friends" or "I cannot pay my bills," then you give yourself an uncalled-for alarm. Those are choices, so you must choose to get up even if it is an effort to do so, choose to job hunt, choose to reach out, and choose to make a budget. How is defeatist thinking helping your well-being? That means you give up before you even start. Sometimes people will choose to stay in their fear and anxiety so they don't have to take any action. Is that you?

Skills to try:

1. Catch what you say to yourself about fear, anxiety, and your "cannots of life" and replace that thought with something realistic. It will help you take your mind off your preoccupation.

2. Can what you are anxious about be solved? If it can't be changed, can you accept it?

3. Fear can be deep-rooted. It may involve other people and their resistance/will. Have patience with yourself and see if a chat with them will help. A chat with people who have overcome fear may be helpful as well.

4. Create a diversion, such as singing, gardening, zoning into a television show, reading, going for a ride, or focusing on favorite things, such as the beach or a hobby. Try an adventure. Don't forget about nature as was just mentioned. Let Mother Nature do her magic.

5. Now your Fear Family. You can't fix them, but you can determine how much time you spend with them. You can set boundaries. Don't take what they say personally. Listen if you can and be helpful if possible but do not get sucked into their fears.

Philippians 4:6–7 (NIV), "Do not be anxious about anything, but in everything, by prayer and petition with thanksgiving, present your requests to God. And the peace of God, which transcends all understanding, will guard your hearts and your minds in Christ Jesus."

Keeping anxiety is like trying to carry one's burden alone. It could be a problem with your faith walk. No condemnation, but consider if there is a gap there in your spiritual walk. Prayer is leaving the requests in the capable hands of God. Thanksgiving is prayer and gratitude for what God has done.

Response:

_____

_____

_____

_____

_____

_____

_____

_____

_____

_____

_____

_____

_____

_____

_____

_____

The Dos and Don'ts to Help Someone Who Has Fear

Whether trying to help a friend or a family member, there are some things that a concerned person can do. There are also things that are not helpful. Fear reminds you to be careful. We like that. We have in our town a forest-like walking trail that divides off into sections. One of those sections has large banana spiders. If helping a person with a fear of spiders, an option can be to take them to a place known to have spiders but only go in for a short way. Well, just letting you know banana spiders have two-inch bodies and three- to four-inch legs with a six-foot web. If it proves to be too much, then maybe choose less intimidating spiders like at the zoo in a glass cage. If a person is choosing to face their fear, someone should be with them. Friends and family sometimes try too much to protect the person, and that does not help them move past fears. Help your person to stay in the present as they may be reliving their fearful event even if it was years ago. They may be embarrassed about their fear, so be kind, encouraging, and supportive.

A thing a concerned person should not do is put pressure on their family or friend. They get to determine their pace. Putting too much pressure on the one you are trying to help could result in the relationship losing its footing. You will need patience, especially if you don't understand their fear. Take their fear seriously. You may not have trouble with enclosed spaces, but your person might. You do not know how difficult it might be to get in the ocean if they once almost drowned or if they can't go out at night due to a negative event. Be compassionate, and don't tell them they are ridiculous or they are a scaredy cat. Also, it can be annoying if you ask too much, "How are you doing?" Let them process their experience and do what the military does: debrief afterward when they feel safe.

Remember setbacks happen. Don't be critical, and don't show your disappointment if they don't make much progress. Do help them remember what progress they have made. If they feel negative about their possible lack of progress, help them not feel overwhelmed. Stay calm yourself, and don't show frustration or anger.

There is a Bible story about a woman named Esther. She risked her life to persuade her husband, King Xerxes, to stop her people, the Jews, from being annihilated. She knew it was against the law to go to the king unless called (even if married to him). She prepared well by asking for all the Jews and her maidens in Shushan to hold a fast. She had faith and trust in God. Esther had people for support as she had a fear she could perish, and it was a very real possibility. She had the weight of the Jewish nation plus her own life and her family's life upon her. I picture her heavily grieved and frightened, trying to keep from showing her internal trembling but, on the other hand, being amazingly brave. The divine providence of God was definitely in effect.

Skill to try:

1. The first two paragraphs have dos and don'ts for helpers. Try those skills if you are going to help someone. If not, then pass the information to another. Remember the suggestion to prepare ahead for helping someone with fear, especially when the magnitude is great as in the story of Esther. Get your own faith and trust where they need to be and get support. Fasting has wonderful benefits as well. I did notice there was no mention of prayer with Esther's story, but it likely occurred, so be sure to pray!

Deuteronomy 3:22 (NIV), "Do not be afraid of them, the Lord your God Himself will fight for you."

Moses was telling Joshua "*your* God" (a personal relationship here) and to not be afraid.

Response:

_____

_____

_____

_____

_____

_____

_____

_____

_____

_____

_____

_____

_____

_____

_____

_____

Stress

Incredible Stress Management

This is the story of the characters from two movies, *The Incredibles*, released in 2004 and 2018. Mrs. Incredible, known as Elastigirl, is a superhero (elasticity/super agility) and a wife and mother of three. She has been irritable and panics or gets angry under pressure but manages to pull it together. Kudos to her for rocking it with her thigh-high boots and tight suit. Ninety percent of us could not pull that off.

Her husband is Mr. Incredible, who has superhuman strength and stamina. He has some life issues. His son, Dash, gets in trouble in school more than once, is frustrated, and likes to bully. The daughter, Violet, is a typical teenager, insecure, and has some parental and sibling conflicts. Jack-Jack is their very busy one-year-old. The family is nice, friendly, strong, caring, and family-oriented.

So what does that have to do with stress? Look at the challenges a regular family has. Well, a family trying to be regular. Mrs. Incredible has some stress trying to balance a career and be a mom. It is a common problem for many of us. She may be missing the accolades that went with her hero career and not getting enough help with the kids. The middle child, Dash, is attention-seeking and craving power. Bullies did not learn kindness or respect. The teenage girl, Violet, could be self-effacing as she experiences loneliness, possibly rejection, does not feel like she has achieved anything, and feels like a disappointment. There are major life stressors, such as moving and going to a new school.

Mr. Incredible has job dissatisfaction, acts like he misses his glory days, and seems bored. He has anger issues—he threw his boss through five walls. If someone is depressed or stressed, they can feel disgruntled, frustrated, and impulsive. He could be angry at the world, angry at events from the past, or angry at himself. After all, he was court-ordered to stop hero work and go into hiding. He definitely has work stress. Mr. Incredible has the signs of going through a midlife crisis. He likely has regrets, maybe feels worthless, sees his achievements are in the past, feels restless, may not feel young, and could be depressed. Sometimes a midlife crisis includes flirting and possibly crossing the line. This man lied, as he wanted to be in control, and likely he did not want to hear what the consequences could be if he told the truth. I am making a point with Mr. Incredible in case you see yourself. He is a good guy. We are all flawed. His real power is that he truly loved his family, and they came together when it counted.

A midlife crisis is not a mental health disorder but rather a transition time or new phase of life. This person between the ages of forty to sixty is evaluating their perception of themself and their life as to what they think they are and what they want to be. It includes a desire to change one's identity. The difference between this transition period and depression is due to the frequency of anxiety and/or low mood. If the person has those feelings here and there, it could be a midlife transition, but with depression the low mood is daily.

Symptoms of a midlife transition are mood swings, change in sleeping patterns, being overly concerned, or not caring about one's appearance and feeling in a rut. They also may include doing a rigorous evaluation of their life, impulsiveness, having a loss of purpose, feeling unfulfilled, feelings of regret, sometimes having physical pain, and loss of interest in leisure activities. The person might believe their best years are behind them; they may indulge in substance abuse and have thoughts of suicide. There is a connection between a midlife transition and affairs. It is more common in men, but both men and women may have a fear of the aging process and their mortality. If you are making major life decisions, such as quitting a job or ending a long-term relationship, then with that bedlam one may need an evaluation with a mental health professional.

Skills to try:

1. If you have stress, pray for insight, talk, and problem-solve before it gets out of hand.

2. Midlife does not have to be a crisis. It can be a wake-up call or a fresh restart. It can be a time to reconnect with family and do fun activities. What do you need to get out of your possible slump? Can it be done realistically?

3. Look at your achievements. Make plans that include your dreams. Find a purpose.

4. Connect with your creative side. At least learn something. Now is the time to take up a sports lesson, painting, writing, pottery, jewelry making, cooking class, dance, music, etcetera, or at least spend time outside. Stay active.

5. Recharge your love life. Share new experiences. Keep things interesting. Show appreciation for each other.

Proverbs 20:29 (NIV), "The glory of young men is their strength, gray hair the splendor of the old."

With age should come experience and wisdom. Young men like to be strong, physically or mentally or both. Older men want to receive honor and respect. Both have value.

Response:

_____

_____

_____

_____

_____

_____

_____

_____

_____

_____

_____

_____

_____

_____

_____

Stress Management Mayo Style

This is not about the creamy condiment but the real deal: the Mayo Clinic. They came up with four points to manage stress. They are reworded to fit the page. The examples and skills are mine for you to consider. The very important thing is to start somewhere to manage all your life happenings so your health and relationships are not damaged.

"Don't stress the could haves, if it should have, it would have" (Unknown).

"The truth is that stress does not come from your boss, your kids, your spouse, traffic jams, health challenges, or other circumstances. It comes from your thoughts about your circumstances" (Andrew Bernstein).

The Mayo Clinic suggests:

1. *Avoid*—you can avoid a lot of stress. Take control of your surroundings. Can you avoid people who stress you out? Learn to say no. Ditch part of your to-do list. Label those things A, B, and C, and on hectic days scratch off C. For example, I say no when necessary, as it helps me make a good decision as well as set a healthy boundary. I also feel like when saying no, nobody is taking undue advantage of me.

2. *Alter*—communicate clearly and let people know your expectations. Respectfully ask someone to alter how they are treating you. Remember to use "I" statements when addressing someone about how you feel. Manage your time better. State your limits in advance. For example, I used to work with people who cursed a lot. I found it necessary to ask them to curb it, as it was disturbing.

3. *Accept*—accepting the situation can ease much of the

stress when avoiding and altering doesn't work. Talk with someone about how you feel. Forgive yourself or others. For example, we all make mistakes, but when someone close to me makes rather big mistakes, I have to accept it was their choice to make. I have to develop tolerance as well.

4. *Adapt*—change standards and expectations of stressful situations. Don't strive for perfection. Choose to focus on the positive aspects of your life. Change your perspective by asking yourself if what is stressing you will matter in five years. For example, in counseling I am blunt, so I expect people to be the same and say what they mean and mean what they say. However, people are not like me, so I have to be patient and open-minded. People are not mind readers.

Mayo also adds the following skills:

1. Think positively. It will help you cope better.

2. Change your emotional response. Even though you can't control some of the stressors in your life, you can control your response to them.

3. Embrace spirituality. Exploring your spirituality can lead to a clear life purpose and better stress management skills.

4. Protect your time. Saying yes to everything comes at a price—more stress and less peace of mind. Learn how to take time for yourself without feeling guilty.

5. Restore work-life balance. Whether the problem is too much focus on work or too little, your work life and personal life feel out of balance. Stress adds harmful physical effects as the result.

6. Try meditation. Different types of meditation techniques can calm your mind and reduce your stress.

7. Keep your cool. If you have a setback, don't give up. Focus on what you can do to gain control of the situa-

tion.

8. Maintain a strong social network. To help you through the stress of tough times, you'll need a strong support network of family, friends, and peers.

Skill to try:

1. Examine each one of the four points above and the eight additional skills. Take each point/skill one at a time and see if adjustments need to be made. As you make positive changes, you are going to like the emerging less-stressed version of yourself.

First Timothy 4:15 (NIV), "Be diligent in these things and give yourself wholly to them, so that your progress will be evident to all."

Be diligent, devoted, and persistent with spiritual disciplines and with getting stress free. Combine diligence with faith, and you should see progress.

Response:

_____

_____

_____

_____

_____

_____

_____

_____

_____

_____

_____

_____

_____

_____

_____

_____

_____

_____

_____

Stress Management Gumby Style

I want another word other than "stress." It's just that there is so much of it and too frequently, even though it is common to all of us. But changing the name will not help you or me. Even if the name was changed to pressure, tension, strain, distress, or hassle, it would still require us all to manage it. One must learn to deal with the things in life that exasperate us, annoy us, irritate us, and cause us anxiety. We just want to be done with all that. Stress, or any of those other names, is like the rubber band; stretch it too much, and it will break, or not enough, and it is rather useless.

Think of Gumby. Do you recall the green clay thing from the 1960s that looked like a large stick of gum? Some of you had not been born yet, but there is a stress management principle here. Maybe his feet were wider so he could stand up. So maybe we can stretch, and we can hold up. We just need some skills to do so.

It sounds like emotional stability. The American Psychological Association defines it as "predictability and consistency in emotional reactions, with absence of rapid mood changes." I would like to order that, please. No, I can't order it; I must work at it. It means that when you find yourself in emotionally challenging situations, you respond in a reasonable, expected way while maintaining composure. So it's about keeping your cool and allowing logic to have a place in your thoughts and behavior. Emotionally stable people tend to be secure, confident, and even-tempered. They exhibit a positive demeanor and get along well with others (Jamie Staudinger).

Can you find some humor in your situation and say, "I am going to be like Gumby or Gumbyetta and stand up and be flexible and resilient"? I had to say Gumbyetta. Maybe that slanted head was extra brains or just a cowlick. Either way, we have enough brains to come up with ways to problem solve and be like the rubber band or clay thing and stretch and stand resolute.

Harvard Business Review did a study and discovered that eighty percent of Americans are stressed at work. The study cited low pay, unreasonable workloads, hectic commutes, and, to a lesser degree, obnoxious coworkers. That was their word, not mine. People seem to bring their home stress to work, and it gets compounded with their work stress, and in the reverse their work stress goes home with them, as the person does not know how to shake it off.

Maria Gonzalez, author of *Mindful Leadership*, reports it is important to train yourself to recognize your "physiological signs of stress." These might be your neck stiffens, your stomach clenches, or your palms sweat. Hormones are being released, which compromises your immune system and your ability to relax. If you recognize the signs, instead of ignoring them, you can start to address the underlying cause of stress. Mine was my blood pressure increased when I went to work and had more than I could get done in my eight hours. I could feel it with a bit of lightheadedness. I had to learn stress management and apply it quickly.

Some skills to try:

1. Talk to trusted friends and spend time with your pets.
2. Don't blow things out of proportion.
3. Makes sure you act, not react. Reacting is responding on impulse rather than acting, which is responding more objectively after the situation has been reviewed.
4. See if your work life and your home life need adjusting, and then do so.

5. Do a pleasant activity daily. Gumby danced with his girlfriend. Aah.

6. That voice in your head might be loud and dogging you. It most likely is informing you, "You can't do this" or "They are messing with you again, giving you a heavy workload." Talk back to the negative voice and counter-act it with something calming. If it is realistically im-possible to get the task done, then be assertive and talk to the boss respectively.

7. Gumby had friends—Prickle, Goo, and Tara and a horse named Pokey. Can you find a trusted person at work or at home who is a good listener who will allow you to "dump" all that tension? I had a friend in the chaplain's office and a few friends who allowed me to call and "unload," as well as I had my dog, Annie. Annie never minded how much I whined, as she got extra walk time out of it. My friends were all very supportive and under-standing through my rough patches. Thank you to all my fabulous friends. I did not dance as Gumby did, but I did sing.

8. Speaking of Gumby's horse Pokey, I would like to ask, have you considered the many benefits of equine thera-py? I have tried this myself at Southern Strides Equine in Cocoa, Florida, after my brother died and have been a counselor watching this work with others. The horse is very intuitive to human emotions. I arrived one time stressed, and the horse backed away from me. That was eye-opening. Horses are very good for the soul.

Second Samuel 6:14 (NIV), "David danced before the Lord with all His might."

Seems like David's dance was one of worship from a man who loved God deeply. He is rejoicing. Besides, dancing releases the "happy hormones," and when the body feels good, the mind does too.

Response:

_____

_____

_____

_____

_____

_____

_____

_____

_____

_____

_____

_____

_____

_____

_____

_____

_____

Stress and Pressure

What is about five pounds but is strong and has longevity? Over time it can get worse. Any guesses? It's a plain old brick. But it's also pressure. They are very much the same. Carry those emotional bricks, that weight, around on your shoulders, and you will feel the pressure. It will certainly show up with your headaches and neck and back aches. Bricks can chip, crack, and crumble. That could be our state if we carried around those kinds of pressure. One five-pound brick can be about finances, another about the children, another about the job stress, the health, and so on. Keep that up, and before long you might have on your shoulders forty pounds of weight. Let's unload. Put the bricks down and make a pathway and step on them.

Hendrie Weisinger, PhD, reports there is a difference between stress and pressure. Amy Morin wrote an article called "Your Failure to Differentiate Stress from Pressure Could Be Your Downfall":

> *Stress refers to the situation of too many demands and not enough resources—time, money, energy— to meet them. Pressure is a situation in which you perceive that something at stake is dependent on the outcome of your performance. Stress can involve a variety of problems that lead to feelings of overload.*

Pressure involves feelings—often of an anxious or fearful nature—of a "do or die" type of situation. An example is you only have one shot at getting it right, such as a presentation. It's you who has to deliver.

You must distinguish if your situation is stress or pressure, as there will be a different course of action. If it is stress, then the goal is to feel less overwhelmed, but if it's pressure, then perform-ing successfully is the goal. To reduce your stress, use stress man-agement, such as walking, to get your endorphins in motion. With pressure, you have to put your energy into performing. This would be like a first responder going to a scene and having to save a life.

> *It is very necessary to know the difference, or else you may go around making little inconveniences feel like a pressure situation. If you walk around con-stantly thinking you're under pressure, you'll believe you have to be successful all the time. You will feel like you are always "under the gun." If you make everything super important, your distress will unnec-essarily intensify.*

Amy Morin

Did you ever wonder how Christ handled stress and pressure? He carried the weight of knowing He would go to the cross and have the sins of the world placed on Him. Really there was no greater weight in all of history. People tried to kill Him; crowds pressed in on Him as well as there were many demands on Him. He was in agony, overwhelmed, and sorrowful. That is extreme physical and mental suffering. Everyone has stress, but Christ was the Prince of Peace and handled things with peace. His pressure buster was He went to a solitary place, got alone with God, His Father, and prayed.

The Word also states Jesus went with three of His disciples to a place called Gethsemane. That tells us that at a time where He was about to undergo the greatest moment in history and expe-rience stress beyond imagination, He had support. Do you think His disciples failed Him a bit by falling asleep on three separate occasions? Or could it be that sleep was their personal coping skill because they were "exhausted from sorrow" (Luke 22:45)? They were human. Sadly, I have been "asleep" when the Lord has asked me to do things. After loss or pending loss, exhaustion is normal. Loss can be traumatic, and it can cause a trauma response in your brain. Support is critical and essential for all of us under stress and pressure.

Skills to try:

1. Lay down those emotional bricks you are carrying. As the Lord modeled this to us, He went to a solitary place, got alone with God, and prayed. He also had support. We know people can let us down, but generally and genuinely, they are there for us.

2. For pressure—plan, prioritize, and don't procrastinate. Have good time management. Evaluate setbacks and readjust new timing if needed.

3. For emergencies—stay calm and help those around you stay calm.

4. Be able to adapt to things out of your control. Focus on what you can control and what needs to be done. Keep the goal in sight.

5. Be aware of your thoughts. Do not allow any thoughts, such as *I can't handle this*, or *This is too hard for me*. It is okay to outsource to others who are better qualified but not because you had negative thinking. You will not be proud of yourself if you do that, and it will not show leadership.

6. For stress—give yourself ten to fifteen minutes for a break to destress. This is good self-care, helps reduce irritability and anxiety, as well as it increases productivity. The mind gets a chance to refocus.

7. To help prevent stress—set boundaries. It lets others know what you are okay with and not okay with. This will help so you are not taken for granted, and it proba-

bly will get you respect.

8. Don't start your day with stress and then arrive at your place of work with that and then take on work stress. Start your day with good nutrition and a positive attitude.

9. Consider that all that multitasking is hard on your brain. It has to focus, then refocus, then focus, and it will drain you. The exception is that being a parent may require you to do multitasking, such as holding a baby, stirring the dinner, and doing homework with another child.

10. Stay away from conflicts and people who just stir up problems. Develop teamwork.

Psalm 119:143 (NIV), "Trouble and distress have come upon me, but your commands are my delight."

Psalm 119 is the longest chapter in the Bible, with 176 verses. It is mostly agreed upon that King David wrote this psalm, and it is a celebration of God's Word and His instruction. If it is King David, he reports he is delighted by God's commands in spite of his troubles. We can adopt this practice of having the word be a delight.

Response:

_____

_____

_____

_____

_____

_____

_____

_____

_____

_____

_____

_____

_____

_____

_____

_____

_____

_____

_____

_____

Stress and Resetting

Let's look at stress from the word "reset." This word is given to you, so when you feel yourself struggling and need a break, you will hopefully use the word and literally do exactly that. Resetting is enabling, rebooting, and retrying after feeling disconnected, drained, or even frustrated. It gives you time to refocus and leave the negative emotions behind. It is taking time to step away and rest and maybe get new ideas, new vision, new goals, new dreams, and new perspectives. Maybe you can examine what your life's purpose is and what gives you meaning. The time you need to reset is up to you. It could be a day or a week; it's your call, as it is your need.

Don't forget in your reset period to examine the bigger picture of where you are spiritually. Consider allowing the Lord to "clear up your challenges" and bring some solutions and transform your thinking. Trust will increase, and stress will decrease. The path before you may have many potholes, and if you stop and look back, you will see the road behind you also had many potholes, but you maneuvered around them. You did it, and you can do it again. Get a visual that the Lord is walking beside you, and He will guide you through. God has a purpose for your life, and when you are trying to find that, don't forget He has His perfect timing to fulfill it.

A person must balance all their multitasking with quiet times and rest to reset. How will you fulfill your calling if you are going in zoom mode most of your day? Even the roadrunner (a member of the cuckoo bird family) may not even be able to catch you. The roadrunner can go at a land speed of about 15 mph and even faster for short bursts. They have long tail feathers that provide balance. That word, "balance," is your key to resetting and, really, life in general. You will need to know what you can change versus what you cannot change. You need to find a balance mentally, socially, physically, relationally, financially, and spiritually to achieve optimum mental health. Give it some serious consideration. It will help you get equilibrium, which is mental balance.

On my reset time, I take on no responsibilities except the ones I want, such as caring for my dog. My time would include a fall mountain view with a porch where I can have a cup of tea and a goodie. It would have my dog near my side. There would have to be a safe hiking path to take in nature. On the porch would be a Chicken Soup for the Soul book, a daily read, my Bible, and a lady's magazine. I would turn on my senses so I could see the beautiful colors, feel the cool mountain air, taste the local bakery fare, hear the rustle of the gold and red leaves as they fall to the ground, and touch the crafts in town, which I would buy. Hope that gives you some ideas. Maybe you reset at the beach or traveling. If there is not a mountain to reset at, I will still go to my porch and walk around the ballfield or the marina. Just find what works for you.

Skills to try:

1. Make your reset time refreshing, fun, and doable. Maybe create a realistic bucket list.
2. Don't lose sight that we are body, soul, and spirit and the spirit needs to develop.
3. This is not time for striving. Really let it go. The first paragraph mentions while you rest, get some new ideas, vision, goals, dreams, and perspective.
4. Do activities that make you smile and feel happy.
5. Examine what could be your purpose and what gives you meaning in life.
6. Have a good understanding of yourself: your needs and

how to meet them when you get back to reality.

7. Take time for yourself, time to be a couple, and to be a family. Make time for friends. This means that you must prioritize the important things. It will be different for everyone.

Psalm 46:10 (NIV), "Be still and know that I am God."

God is saying to stop striving and relax. Just be in awe of God, who is sovereign and in control.

Response:

_____

_____

_____

_____

_____

_____

_____

_____

_____

_____

_____

_____

_____

Anger

Anger Is Like Quicksand

Quicksand is sand that behaves like a liquid because it is saturated with water. When it is disturbed, it becomes unstable. The person who happens to enter into the quicksand may have a feeling they are now trapped. With any length of time, depending on the elements, the person who can't extricate themself from it can have a sunstroke, be dehydrated, have hypothermia, drown, or be attacked by an animal. National Geographic did a piece called "Can You Survive Quicksand?" (YouTube, March 2013), where an experiment was done with a man who volunteered to get in quicksand to see what would happen. The man entered the quicksand, and it took only eight minutes for him to sink to his waist. He became "stuck fast" and asked to be rescued. He stated he felt scared, helpless, and uncomfortable as anybody would.

So what does this have to do with anger? The comparison is the person with an anger issue will stay "stuck" with that anger or aggression until skills are learned and applied to "free" themself. In the case of getting free from quicksand, one needs to lie back, stay in the supine position, and let the body float with face and torse up. If a person panics, they could sink further. A person in that situation must stay calm. You make slow movements of the legs to increase the viscosity of the fluid. The angry individual is the opposite of calm. The angry person may be "struggling" by expressing themself physically by throwing things, hitting things, or clenching their fist, or maybe it's all verbal, such as swearing and yelling. Being calm is something that needs to be learned. Anger is a learned behavior, and thus, skills can be learned to gain self-restraint.

With anger a person feels overwhelmed and stressed and that something is out of control. This person will most likely have anxiety and frustration because they do not know how to handle their circumstance, their "quicksand." With anger a person may feel "emotionally imprisoned" by irritation, fear, excitement, pain, or anxiety. With anxiety a person may feel "cornered" by what will happen next, and it can lead to panic and feeling "trapped" by fear and loss of control. These three cousins, anxiety, panic, and anger, cause very uneasy feelings and low tolerance to deal with the situation. It's okay to feel anxiety and fear about uncertainty but managing it is, of course, best.

Let's get you out of your vexed lifestyle before you sink in your anger quicksand. I want you to live to a ripe old age, not prematurely die from the effects of anger. There is a higher risk for cardiovascular disease for individuals with anger and aggression. It is especially true for those who are chronically angry, those who frequently and intensely let their anger disrupt their lives.

Anger will most assuredly cause you to not be proud of who you are. I can't see an angry person feeling good about themself or really enjoying life. Sometimes the anger one spews on another is misguided, as that person may think it gets them respect. However, it only serves to make people not want to be around you due to your lack of self-control. If your goal was to make people afraid

190

of you, then you may have accomplished that, but who really likes an irate bully? Nobody ever says, "It's going to be a great day, as I get to spend time with Furious Fiona or Exasperated Earl." You might put people on eggshells. Don't expect others to answer your call when they see your name on their caller ID. Trust is hard to regain after an angry tirade. Promotions would most likely go to the worker who is respected. When you come home from work, you would not want your spouse or children to say, "Oh no, Dad (or Mom) is home," and retreat to their bedroom as a safe haven because they don't want to deal with you and your agitation. That would be a sad commentary on the family life.

Skills to try:

1. When you feel like things are building up, create some physical distance between you and what is upsetting you. Go and unwind. A time-out is however long you need.

2. If the concern is with you and another person, and you have dealt with your own trigger and cooled off, then see if you can cool off your opponent. Look at the other person's point of view. Ask yourself if it is really serious enough to be mad over. Ask yourself if what has you steamed is really about that or something else. For example, I had a boss who was grumpy with every employee, including me. It seemed like none of us were doing anything to deserve her ire. One day I simply asked her kindly what was wrong, and she said that she had been diagnosed with cancer and she did not think her marriage would survive it. She was much nicer to only me after I offered her some empathy.

3. Listen to the other person. They have a side of the story as well. They have needs and wants too. See if you can restrain your anger to an appropriate time that does not have an audience, like not in a business meeting. Espe-

cially don't "blow" in front of the children, as they do not need to be involved in adult affairs. Respect is lost, and fear can result. Time and place are everything. Stay cool until then, and continue to be cool so you can resolve the issues.

4. People who are learning anger management have a word they say to themselves to buy time for the blood to circulate from the heart, through the body, and back to the heart. This allows about forty-five seconds to cool down, so the brain performs more clearly and before something is said or done that is full of regrets. Your buzz words can be simple, such as "cool down," "easy does it," "relax," "be at peace," or "chill, Bill."

Proverbs 15:1 (NIV), "A gentle answer turns away wrath, but a harsh answer stirs up anger."

A gentle answer toward an angry person may just be the water they need to put out the fire.

Response:

_____

_____

_____

_____

_____

_____

_____

_____

_____

_____

_____

_____

_____

_____

_____

_____

_____

_____

_____

_____

Something Bad Happened to You

Before dealing with childhood trauma, let me tell you about a butterfly's struggle to be released from its cocoon. The struggle is so intense that it will appear that it is close to death. Nobody should rescue it, as the butterfly needs to do so itself. The butterfly releases a chemical that strengthens its wings so they can expand. Timing is everything; too early, and they are doomed, as they will not have developed enough. It will look small and crumpled. The butterfly needs to "hang down" so its wings can expand and it can dry. The butterfly will stay like that for about eighteen hours. We are like this; we may have to go through a struggle to emerge and be able to fly with life. A person having gone through trauma has certainly been "hanging down." Never lose sight of the fact that the Lord is present in our efforts to emerge from where we have been encased.

This is about childhood trauma and its connection to anger. Childhood trauma is often described as a serious adverse childhood experience (ACEs). It is expected that an adult is reading this, and it may or may not be you who had the childhood trauma. Trauma is complex, but there is help. Childhood trauma is a frightening, dangerous, violent, or life-threatening event that happens to a child. Research reports that 65 percent of children experience at least one adverse event during their childhood, and nearly 40 percent of children experience at least two or more ACEs. The greater number of ACEs a child has been exposed to, the greater the child will be at risk for developing physical or mental problems throughout their lifespan. For example, heart and lung disease, alcoholism, risk for intimate partner violence, drug use, poor academic performance, depression, and suicide (Center for Child

Trauma Assessment, Services and Intervention).

Anger and trauma are very much connected. Ask yourself whether or not you experienced physical, sexual, or emotional abuse or physical or emotional neglect. Did you witness violence of anyone, not just a family member or friend? In the immediate household, was there any mental illness, substance abuse, or separation? Was there a change of caregiver, such as foster care, a death, or was someone incarcerated? Were you a victim of being bullied or in a serious accident? In all likelihood, your anger could be coming from those experiences.

Now consider your behaviors. Are you angry, depressed, anxious, or hypervigilant? Do you have trouble controlling your emotions in general, feel disconnected, or have trouble relating to others? Sometimes those who have childhood trauma cannot explain why they react to certain people negatively. Possibly your self-esteem is low. Usually, the victim of childhood trauma struggles to resolve conflicts appropriately. Add on fear, guilt, and shame. The potential for personality disorders can manifest. Post-traumatic stress can develop. Intrusive thoughts can happen and be problematic as well as one can have nightmares and visual images of the traumatic event. There may be memory lapses. Stress seems to make things worse and has long-term symptoms, such as health problems. High-risk behaviors are engaged in more than usual.

In relationships a person may feel like their significant other will harm them even if there is no evidence to back that up. The individual still feels vulnerable and will likely have trouble trusting. The person's sense of security is almost null and void. Fears of abandonment surface.

Although it would seem like all the above paragraphs are a

story of doomsday, that is far from the truth. Your story is not finished, and God is not finished with you either. God does not waste the events that happen in one's life. He is excellent in helping you become what He sees you can become.

The statistics are that if you meet five people, three of them will have a history of childhood trauma. So there is a major common denominator. Just think that if that many people have grown up with trauma, there are many who can relate to you as well as you may be a catalyst to help somebody else. The big thing to keep in mind is you survived.

If you come from a household where there was a significant amount of caregiver dysfunction, or you were the victim, there is always hope. If anything, it will tell you what you do not want for your life. I expect you will work hard to see to it that you overcome your negative history and be the parent who raises their children in a healthy and happy environment. If the childhood trauma is serious and you are struggling to self-manage, I recommend therapy.

Skills to try:

1. Grieve the loss of your childhood.
2. Take good care of yourself now.
3. Acknowledge your feelings. Your feelings matter, and you matter.
4. As hard as this is, let go of the past and move forward one step at a time to a life you deserve.
5. Set boundaries up and distance yourself from those who hurt you.
6. Reach out for help. Be heard, be understood, and be validated.
7. Interrupt any angry, negative, or critical thoughts you are saying about yourself. Put up a mental stop sign

when you catch yourself saying things like, "You are stupid or worthless." Ask yourself if it is your thought or what you were told as a child. Ask yourself how you know that is true. Believe good things about yourself.

8. Release anger that is pent up in your body by doing something physical.

9. Get support. They can help alleviate the stress and help you work toward wholeness. They can teach coping skills. The support system can help you recognize your triggers, give you feedback, and help you stay on track. They can be someone who holds you accountable.

James 1:19–20 (NIV), "Everyone should be quick to listen, slow to speak and slow to become angry, for man's anger does not bring about the righteous life that God desires."

Listen, then listen some more. We get so much further in our relationships and our witness to others when we listen more than talk. Some people "talk at others." I can't see that working. I personally tune someone out who does that to me. It comes across as disrespectful, manipulative, or that person is a know-it-all. We need God's help to control our tongues. What is down in the well (deep inside of us) comes up in the bucket (out our mouths). The question could be asked, "What does one's anger produce?" I would say probably not the righteous life.

Response:

_____

_____

_____

_____

_____

_____

_____

_____

_____

_____

_____

_____

_____

_____

_____

_____

_____

_____

Hothead Horatio Meet Angry Angie

Wait, let me think about that. Maybe that is not such a good idea—having two people with anger issues in a relationship. Well, it is most common, though. For people who have not learned how to manage their emotions, damage can be done, and lasting scars can occur. Without learning how to be angry in a healthy way or to even fight fairly, it would become hard to trust again. It will certainly increase your anxiety and blood pressure.

Anger is a strong feeling of displeasure with someone or something, combined with an urge to fight. Anger and fear are two basic emotions. The fear, which is really anxiety, usually makes a person want to run away, and the anger makes one want to fight back. This can come with a cost to themselves.

Do you feel like anger is a normal emotion? We all feel angry at times. It's energy. It is not good or bad. It is a natural reaction to being threatened or attacked. So expressing anger may sometimes be healthy, but losing control is not.

There are reasons to keep anger in. Some are that one's health is affected, there could be hurt feelings, misunderstandings, a relationship can be broken, and it could result in trouble with the law. If a person is known as a "hothead," then a negative reputation has developed, and hence there are the possibilities of lost opportunities for doing activities and employment.

On the flip side, there are valid reasons to express anger. It may keep a person from "blowing their top." Anger, being energy, helps in the case of an emergency as well, as you can get things done. Letting anger out appropriately lets another person know they are doing something you don't like, and it is having a strong effect on you. Catch the word appropriately.

What makes one person angry may not be the same for another and to the same degree. Why does someone get road rage and another is calm for the same scenario? Another case is a messy house can easily upset one person, and to another it is just the way it is when having a hectic day with the children. Items that get lost bother one person, but to another they are treated like it is no problem. Some people get upset when there is disorganization or they are not treated fairly. There is the life stuff like the toilet that does not get flushed, the child who has a messy diaper, or the spouse who interrupts at a moment you need your space. There is the game in which a player flubs an important play, and the reaction includes some explicit words. It's about what is going on emotionally. Is there existing depression, anxiety, fear, or loneliness, and the next thing that happens is "the last straw"? There are a host of little and big annoyances that happen to us all.

However, what makes a person go from one to ten so quickly? It's all about anger triggers. That is a sensitive area in your emotions that gets stirred up by a certain situation, person, topic, etcetera. The things you experience in life train your brain to react in certain ways (Ipseity Counseling).

Triggers are external and internal. External triggers are things that other people say or do that you feel angry about, such as someone stealing from you or people talking about you behind your back. Internal triggers are things you choose to say to yourself that cause you to get angry. An example is "Why did I do that? I am so stupid" or "She is laughing at me; I'll get back at her." Notice you chose to get angry.

Back to Hothead Horatio and Angry Angie. If you learn what triggers your anger, you can apply skills so you can get to a point of healing. Look at the triggers in a relationship. Examine possibilities from this list: Do you feel like your partner does or says things that you find inconsiderate or unfair? What if the other person is always late? Do you feel important? Does it seem like work comes first? Are you struggling with the person not sharing household responsibilities? Is your partner financially responsible? Are your and the partner's priorities aligned? Does your significant other hold grudges that cause you to feel like you can't ever be forgiven? (Talkspace, January 4, 2022).

There are more to consider. Is there a trigger about a past relationship? Virtually anything about an ex-partner can be a trigger, such as that person's past and current behavior, how much they want to connect with their ex currently, what things they shared together, and the family or friends that are mutual. Is your partner lying about their ex? Are the expectations you had with the ex the same as for you? Is it causing current disputes or lack of respect? Are there disappointments? Are you being respected?

Skills to try:

1. Get yourself calm first, and then you can express your feelings. Decompress. If you are trying to communicate when angry, you will not be thinking straight and will say things you will be sorry for as well as probably make things escalate. Choose to be focused and to chill out. Tell yourself that nobody has the power to bring you to that much anger unless you give them the power. Even if someone is pulling your chain and they want you to lose it, don't give your power away, or they win, and you lose.

2. In trying to be aware of your own triggers, make a list of what triggers you. Now ask yourself, "Why does this cause such a high emotional reaction?"

3. Answer the questions from the paragraphs above for more self-enlightenment.

Ephesians 4:31 (NIV), "Get rid of all bitterness, rage and anger, brawling and slander, along with every form of malice."

There should be no anger, violence, rage, fighting, quarreling in a loud way, making false statements, or any intent of evil. Forgiveness helps to bring these intense emotions to an end. We need to love in the way Christ loved us. We have things to work on.

Response:

_____

_____

_____

_____

_____

_____

_____

_____

_____

_____

_____

_____

_____

_____

Understanding and Helping the Angry Child

Try this trivia before you dive into anger in children. What begins to show dominance or aggression about the age of seven? This mammal has a record of killing, on average, five hundred people a year. It wants to kill people but does not want to eat them. Some of that killing is done by its very large incisor teeth and lower canine teeth, which never stop growing. The aggression comes from being highly territorial. What mammal do you think this big angry beast is? It is a hippopotamus.

Anger is a normal, healthy emotion if expressed appropriately. For some, anger is survival. By that the child is just trying to cope and survive, and their anger makes them feel powerful. However, some children do not realize that the angry feeling they are experiencing has turned into aggression. Aggression is an indicator that feelings have become extreme and interfere with daily living.

When children are angry, there could be an underlying mental health issue, such as attention deficit hyperactivity disorder (ADHD), autism, obsessive-compulsive disorder (OCD), anxiety, or even Tourette syndrome. Bipolar disorder, called a mood disorder, usually develops in older teenagers and young adults but has on rare occasions been diagnosed in younger children. The symptom would be primarily mania, which triggers aggressive emotions and anger. The racing thoughts can leave one irritable and frustrated. If there are consistent problems in school, then there could be a learning disorder. For the child who is strong-willed or oversensitive or one who has trouble processing sensory information, then frustration and anger would be common. Not only could there be hidden mental health issues, but there could be health issues such as unstable blood sugar or the results of improper diet or lack of sleep.

Anger in children can also be caused by frustration or distress, as the child does not get what they want or just doesn't want to do what is asked of them. Some children have unresolved feelings, such as grief due to a death or their caregiver's absence, possibly due to addiction, divorce, incarceration, or other family trauma. If a parent is away in the military, mission field, or on business, then the child may be angry at the parent for leaving.

Being put in the foster care system can cause great distress, which can lead to fear and anger. If a child has been bullied or abused, they can be angry, depressed, anxious, or all three. If the child has witnessed violence, they are at a higher risk for depression, anxiety, and fighting. With any negative history, the child likely will have low frustration tolerance. This means they are easily frustrated by everyday inconveniences. Family dysfunction and parents that have a hard parenting style, such as authoritarian or even neglectful, can cause a child to struggle to regulate their own emotions. If the child is feeling disconnected from their parent, they may act out to let someone know they need to feel secure and loved.

Signs that a child's emotional outburst should be of concern come from the Child Mind Institute. They are:

1. If your child's tantrums and outbursts are occurring past the age in which they're developmentally expected (up to about seven or eight years old).
2. If their behavior is dangerous to themselves or others.
3. If their behavior is causing them serious trouble in school, with teachers reporting that they are out of control.

4. If their behavior is interfering with their ability to get along with other kids, so they're excluded from play dates and birthday parties.

5. If their tantrums and defiance are causing a lot of conflict at home and disrupting family life.

6. If they're upset because they feel they can't control their anger, and it makes them feel bad about themselves.

You have just read of the many possible causes of anger in children, but consider starting with a checkup with a doctor who can, at that time, also determine if there is a need for a counselor.

Skills to try:

1. Parent management training is beneficial. Skills are taught that help the parent manage their angry child.

2. Model good self-control. You can verbalize your feelings and teach your child why you got upset. Personally, I get annoyed when I hear a parent swearing at their child. I also was disgusted at a former neighbor who decided to rant and rave at the children's mother in front of the children.

3. Teach your child what is acceptable, such as "We don't call each other names" and "We don't throw things or break things." Teach, "We don't hurt anyone or destroy property, and we don't yell at each other." Teach and model manners.

4. There is an excellent resource for you to teach calm-down skills for children and teens at www.andnext-comesl.com. There are many resources out there, so please avail yourself to them, but this one had a unique way of teaching breathing skills and how to make a "calm down" kit.

5. Try and find the triggers so you can help your child problem-solve. Overstimulation and frustration are common ones. Disappointment, fatigue, and hunger can be triggers. Maybe a friend did not give the child a birthday

invitation, or a bully is bothering your child. Trouble with math or reading can be a trigger. If you know ahead of time that a situation causes your child to be triggered, then go with plan B or problem-solve ahead of time. For example, noise can be a problem for kids on the autism spectrum.

6. Always be an active listener and be patient. After an angry episode, teach your child to ask themself why they were angry, what they did, what worked, and what didn't work. Ask what they would do differently next time and how it felt in their body.

7. For low frustration tolerance, teach that life will have inconveniences and things will go wrong, but that it is temporary.

Ephesians 6:4 (NIV), "Fathers, do not exasperate your children; instead, bring them up in the training and instruction of the Lord."

Fathers, and it applies to mothers as God is no respecter of person, are not to be a source of agitation or irritation to their children. Parents do this by showing their own temper or, for that matter, any negative behavior, neglecting their children, or any mental, physical, or emotional abuse. We are to show our children by example by modeling and teaching them what is right and teaching about the Lord.

Response:

_____

_____

_____

_____

_____

_____

_____

_____

_____

_____

_____

_____

_____

_____

_____

_____

_____

_____

_____

Understanding and Helping
the Angry Teenager

To my children:

If you need me, just call me. I don't care if I'm asleep. If I'm angry with you or if I'm having my own problems—just call me. I will always be there for you, no matter how big or small your problem is, I will be there.

This saying by an unknown source says a lot when it comes to teens and their problems. Another quote I like is:

"My child is not giving me a hard time, my child is having a hard time" (Unknown).

I expect at times you wanted to keep your teenager away from civilization until they could get through the tumultuous adolescence period. One thing that is needed is to understand that their brain is not fully developed yet, so those "absurd" decisions they sometimes make are legit in the sense that their prefrontal cortex is still growing. The prefrontal cortex is the decision-making center, the rational part, and the last part of the brain to mature. Teenagers process information with the amygdala, which is the emotional part rather than the rational part. This developmental process is completed about by the age of twenty-five.

That should explain a lot. I once saw two young teenagers at one of our local parks trying to entice an alligator to come to them. We all know of teens who have decided to attend a party and get drunk or high with little regard for the consequences. We all also know teenagers who involve themselves in risky behaviors due to the same ineptitude for self-control. Unprotected sex, fast-speed driving, illegal activity, or self-harm are other examples. The brain that is not fully developed is not an excuse I would give to the teens, but this fact should help a parent who wants to talk to their teens about their impulsive behaviors and consequences.

There are numerous reasons for anger in teenagers. Poor self-esteem is a big one. The cause of this may be family disharmony or lack of parental support, friends who are a bad influence, stressful life experiences, school adjustment, and so much focus on body image, particularly for girls. Teenage boys are much more likely to be angry when they have an underlying mental health condition, such as depression, anxiety, bipolar disorder, or other condition. There could be other concerns, such as substance abuse or a history of trauma. The teen may feel unloved and insecure, or there has been a death of someone the teen loved. The family itself could be modeling negative anger responses due to their own personal maladjustment.

Sometimes the teen is angry to protect themselves from disclosing vulnerable emotions. Anger helps them feel empowered with a sense of control. It helps them soothe numbing pain, and it is used to push parents away emotionally while getting undivided attention (Leon Seltzer, PhD, Psychology Today).

A parent needs to look for any secondary emotions that could be covering up an underlying issue, such as fear, shame, hurt, pain, or depression. If these emotions become too much, the teen may fly off the handle. If anger becomes out of control and it is too frequent, if there is excessive arguing, violence, threats, cruel behaviors, or destruction, a mental health professional should be consulted.

Teens are changing physically, mentally, and socially, and they need coping skills to help them maneuver all the adjustments. They will need skills to be able to express their anger in healthy ways. You may think you can breathe a sigh of relief that you got them to their eighteenth birthday, but remember the brain is still maturing into their twenties.

Skills to try:

1. Listen to your teen and let them know you are there for them. Love them unconditionally. They will need to hear this and be shown this. Create a sense of belonging. When you listen, see if you can discover what is really bothering them. It may be that your teen did not get picked for the team or did not get asked for a date. Don't judge. It's their immature emotions.

2. Your teen may feel moody and be unpredictable, so pick your battles. Do not choose to fight every problem or involve yourself in every argument. Get involved in what is important; otherwise, it could be exhausting, and there could be damage to your relationship.

3. Teach your teen how to regulate their emotions. Not only do they have the immature brain, but they have hormones that go berserk. This will require they learn how to soothe their own emotions and even others' and identify what they are feeling and what others are feeling. They will need to build resilience and confidence, self-control, and to hold up under peer pressure.

4. Set boundaries. Rules and consequences help the teen know you care for their welfare and want to keep them safe. An example is a curfew or restriction from certain places.

5. Spend time with your teenager. Do something they are interested in.

6. Make sure they get a good eight to ten hours of sleep a night, eat right, have a solid exercise routine that helps burn off anger and energy, and have healthy hobbies.

Have meals and table conversations with your teen.
Know who their friends are.

Malachi 4:6 (NIV), "He will turn the hearts of the fathers to their children, and the hearts of the children to their fathers."

This includes mothers, as God is no respecter of persons. Pray this verse when things have become estranged in the parent-child relationship. The Greek version of this verse translates as "restore," and the Hebrew version translates to "reconcile." Keep hope alive. God loves to repair our families to bring them to Himself and to each other.

Response:

_____

_____

_____

_____

_____

_____

_____

_____

_____

_____

_____

_____

Unforgiveness

Please Don't Be Like a Corvid

Are you looking up the word "corvid"? I had to look it up. It is a bird in the crow family. The crow is my example of unforgiveness. Did you know crows can hold a grudge and can be vindictive? A University of Washington wildlife biologist, Dr. John Marzluff, did an experiment on crows in which he and two students wore ugly, dangerous-looking masks and one wore a neutral mask. Those in dangerous-looking masks captured some crows, studied them, and then released them. Those doing the experiment who wore the ugly masks found that as they walked around the campus, the crows had not forgotten the captors who wore the ugly masks. They even chastised the ugly mask-wearing people. In one particular walk, Professor Marzluff was scolded by forty-seven out of fifty-three crows. The neutral mask had very little effect. The hypothesis is that crows learn to recognize threatening humans (*The New York Times*, Michelle Nijhuis, August 25, 2008).

When a crow encounters a "mean" human, they will even teach other crows to identify that alleged mean human. Crows will band together and chase predators. This could be considered paltry, but it shows how intelligent they are and that they have good survival skills. They have learned how to avoid the people who would harm them.

What does all this have to do with unforgiveness? The behavior of the crows to their captors or predators is a very similar behavior of humans who have chosen not to forgive. The comparison is humans can be revengeful, relentless, and resentful. They can be protestors and squawkers. Humans, like crows, don't forget either.

Forgiveness is excusing a fault, canceling the expected payment for a wrong, and giving up any right to hurt someone who hurt us. It is a process where a person acknowledges their hurt but drops the case. It is about extending mercy even when the offender does not deserve it. We do not need to forgive the offense, but we need to leave it in God's hands and move on. Vengeance belongs to the Lord. We are not to "settle the score." Criminal cases should be left to the justice system. Do not condone the offender's actions. We also do not need to have a relationship with the offender, especially if it is someone who is dangerous for you or your family to be around or they are pressuring you into negative or unlawful behavior.

Sometimes it is just a necessity to distance oneself from toxic relationships, and that includes family who has caused harm and great hurt. There is nothing wrong with taking time to heal. Separation can be helpful. Some people in one's life need to be in the past and stay there. Still, the hard process of choosing to forgive is of utmost importance. I said process because it is an undertaking. There are steps to take to get to a happy life in which you do not look at your life through a lens of hurt and suffering. You do not deserve to forever ache. You are worthy of being whole again.

To give you a personal story of the people I have had to forgive and the list of their misdeeds would be like "throwing them under the bus." I won't do that. Forgiveness was given, but trust had to be earned. With some things it took a few years to rebuild trust. One person had to show me they were worthy of being trusted again. I received counseling and asked God to step into my crises. I accepted support and prayer from my pastors and from a dozen beloved friends who prayed for me through it all. I trusted God first and then, at my pace, regained trust with those who caused me emotional and financial harm. My self-esteem over the years had taken a big hit, and it needed to recover. I am appreciative of the kind words from Pastor John C., who describes me now with three special words: sweet, grateful, and strong. That means so much. I got there, and so can you. Pick your three empowering words. You can pick more if you want.

I worked for the sheriff in my county for the last fifteen years and, previous to that, two mental health facilities, a juvenile detention facility, as well as the school board as a teacher. Somehow, when you let the Lord have all those overwhelming, stressful events, He is able to use those rueful situations and put you in the position to help others heal. I liked my job with the sheriff's department, but the stories that I was told while working with inmates were often quite disturbing. You had to have broad shoulders and shake them off before getting home. I rose to the occasion and offered those clients a lot of help with how to apply coping skills and not repeat those destructive behaviors again. You are receiving the benefit of learning many coping skills throughout this book to move forward.

Skills to try:

1. The One who is our example of forgiveness is Jesus Christ. He paved the way for us to not have to go to hell. Examine where you are spiritually and see if you need

to talk to the Lord.

2. First you need to see the importance of asking for forgiveness. It can heal your deep wounds. Forgiveness
   can decrease depression, anxiety, hostility, bitterness,
   hardness, and even post-traumatic stress. It can improve
   self-esteem. It can improve relationships and physical
   health.

3. Find meaning in your suffering. Hopelessness tries to
   creep in. Anguish and adversity change people, but if
   you look for the positive, you will feel stronger and
   more resilient.

4. Do not allow yourself to stay in a role as a victim. This
   will help you not feel like the offender has power over
   you. Feeling like a victim keeps you reliving the negative moments.

5. The crow is an intelligent and beautiful creation. Let
   yourself heal and be patient through the process so you
   can feel like that—a beautiful and intelligent creation,
   not one harboring unforgiveness.

6. I will never minimize how traumatic your circumstance
   may have been. If it has been too much for you and you
   have little to no support, then therapy is recommended.

Matthew 6:14–15 (NIV), "If you forgive men when they sin
against you, your heavenly Father will also forgive you. If you do
not forgive men their sins, your Father will not forgive your sins."

It means what it says. To receive God's forgiveness, one must
be willing to forgive others.

Response:

_____

_____

_____

_____

_____

_____

_____

_____

_____

_____

_____

_____

_____

_____

_____

_____

_____

_____

A Very Wise Jenny

There are many biblical stories about forgiveness. I decided not to use the more famous ones like the prodigal son, Joseph and his brothers, King David, or Paul. Let's take a look at Balaam's donkey in Numbers 22 and how that connects to forgiveness. The king of Moab wanted the Israelites cursed, so he hired Balaam, a prophet, to do just that. God did not allow Balaam to go and curse the people who He had blessed. The king of Moab sweetened the pot by offering greater rewards. Balaam got on his donkey and went, but God was angry. God sent an angel to divert Balaam from the path. En route, Balaam's donkey saw that angel with a drawn sword, so she turned off the road into a field. The result was Balaam beat her. The next occurrence when the donkey saw the angel of the Lord was going through a narrow path and the donkey pressed close to a wall, so Balaam beat her, as his foot was injured. The third time was when the donkey had no room to turn, so she lay down, and Balaam was angry and beat her with his staff.

I am calling this donkey Jenny because it means a female donkey. In Hebrew the interpretation means "gracious" or "merciful." This donkey was indeed a description of that. She needs this lovely name, as she has been through a lot. I am also calling this story animal cruelty. As the story unfolded, the donkey asked Balaam, "What have I done to you to make you beat me these three times?" Instead of being shocked that his donkey was talking to him, he replied to Jenny's question, "You have made a fool of me! If I had a sword in my hand, I would kill you right now."

Donkeys are faithful animals. As the narrative ended, Balaam was shown the angel of the Lord and given an explanation. Jenny most likely forgave her mean owner, as animals do that. They are benevolent. Never doubt that God sees what you have been through or are currently going through. He sees every detail and is on the scene whether you sense His presence or not. Jenny saw and acted accordingly, saving her master's life. The angel of the Lord is speaking in Numbers 22:33 (NIV), "If she had not turned away, I would have certainly killed you by now, but I would have spared her."

Always keep in mind we are to forgive, but we leave room for God's wrath. If you try and pursue revenge for all the "abuse" you encountered, it would be like saying God can't do His job. Oh no! Forgiving someone does not mean the elimination of consequences. There could be a health scare, a job loss, divorce, jail, and a host of ways God avenges. It is up to God, and He is sovereign. You may find this interesting that in Joshua 13:22 it records that the Israelites killed Balaam with a sword.

Particularly with family and friendships, there should be a desire for healing and forgiveness, not vengeance. We may need to take a risk and trust again, knowing the possibility exists we can be hurt again. Trust your intuition. Listen to the Lord. People have a tendency to relive over and over the suffering and how they were wronged. That futile exercise of the mind and heart will never bring you rest and relief. Forgive and be able to call it "over and done with." The French word for finished is *fini*. It can be your buzzword when hurtful emotions attempt a comeback. Say, "It is *fini!*"

Granting forgiveness does not mean you are granting trust. It does not mean the offender is off the hook. Forgiveness is not about the other person. Forgiveness is a gift you give yourself so you are free from bitterness, resentment, and hurt. It's about getting your peace back. Try wrapping a box and calling it "the gift of forgiveness." Wrap it in your favorite paper and put a lovely bow on it, then give it to yourself. Maybe you can include a letter in the gift box that states how you were hurt due to the betrayal (you fill in the blank) and that it made you feel disrespected, deeply hurt, and unloved (you fill in the feelings). Say you cannot change the past and that you are letting it all go now. Tell yourself you have self-respect, self-love, and peace now (you fill in the blank). End with "I am choosing to forgive you (fill in the offender's name)" and that you are moving on. You get to choose to keep the box or discard it. Keeping it may be a good reminder that you do not feel the anger or as much anger or deep hurt anymore and have moved onto full control of your life, which includes peace and happiness.

Skills to try:

1. Try making a gift box for yourself. I really expect you will find it liberating.

2. You do not have to agree by any means with what was done, but consider putting yourself in the other person's shoes. It might even be weird I am suggesting that. Consider if there were extenuating circumstances, such as they were distraught over something and would ordinarily never behave in that manner. Was it out of character for the offender? Was it an isolated incident? Did a loved one die, or was there another tragedy and they were not in their right mind? Were they high, drunk, or in pain? Is their health or medication off-kilter? Were they exhausted, and thus they might have had brain fog? Was there a negative influence when the offender was vulnerable? Does that person have some past of their own that still needs healing? Is there a benefit of the doubt you can offer? In the cases of abuse or trauma that was particularly difficult, a therapist can be a good support.

3. If the other person does not seek forgiveness, remember

you are in control of only yourself.

4. Do you need to make plans for self-protection? Call the Domestic Abuse Hotline at 1–800–799–7233 or text START to 88788.

Colossians 3:13 (NIV), "Bear with each other and forgive whatever grievance you may have against each other. Forgive as the Lord forgives you."

At times there will be people we can't get along with, or the issue can't be resolved. It's understandable. Abuse, trauma, and many other life events carry the potential to hurt the heart deeply, and I will never downplay the crushing impact on you. Jesus has forgiven us so much that Paul was just trying to express we should forgive others.

Response:

_____

_____

_____

_____

_____

_____

_____

_____

_____

_____

_____

_____

_____

_____

_____

_____

_____

_____

_____

Jeremiah Was Not a Bullfrog

There was a very popular song in 1970 done by Three Dog Night and written by Hoyt Axton; its opening line was "Jeremiah was a bullfrog." However catchy that line was, it was not about a bullfrog. I have a comparison, though, and that is—grudges are like bullfrogs. Read to see why.

A grudge is when you harbor anger, bitterness, resentment, or other negative feelings long after someone has done something to hurt you.

What are some telltale signs that you are harboring a grudge? Insider.com reports these:

1. When you are holding a grudge, all sorts of things can cause you to get frustrated. You may find yourself taking advantage of every opportunity to be heard. You may have a grudge against someone but pretend like things are fine, then an unrelated issue may set you off.

2. Avoidance may be a sign that you are holding a grudge.

3. You still feel bitter. You have not moved forward without feeling embittered or angry.

4. When you think about the other person, your feelings are negative.

5. If you are mostly concerned with the other person understanding where you were coming from and ensuring that they see your side of things.

6. You feel nothing, or you feel indifferent. You have chosen to be emotionally detached and uninterested.

7. You cancel plans at the last minute. The feeling that causes you to want to back out is likely a resentment lurking beneath the surface.

8. It's easy to get irritated with the person.

Esau and Jacob are twin brothers in the book of Genesis. Esau was born first. Isaac, their father, was close to dying, so the plan was to give Esau his blessings before he died. The custom was when a father died and his inheritance was divided, the first-born was to get a "double portion." The twin's mother, Rebekah, schemed with the twin brother Jacob to disguise him as Esau to get the blessing. Isaac had poor eyesight, so he was tricked into giving his blessings to Jacob. Esau was very angry. Esau held a grudge against Jacob and said to himself, in Genesis 27:41 (NIV), "The days of mourning for my father are near; then I will kill my brother Jacob." Rebekah heard about this plot and, with her own agenda, had Jacob sent away on the premise of finding a wife. Many years passed, and Jacob and Esau decided to reconnect, and a location was agreed upon. Jacob sent Esau hundreds of animals, possibly as restitution for the blessing that he stole. Jacob approached slowly and bowed, and Esau ran to him and embraced him. They wept. Esau forgave Jacob for the trickery.

People will forever in our life disappoint because they are not perfect, and we all have problems. In the case of grudges and these two brothers, I would say don't nurse, rehearse, curse, coerce, or immerse yourself in the situation that caused your old wounds.

Back to Jeremiah, our so-named bullfrog. A male bullfrog has a call that is deep and loud, and they hunt under the guise of dark to get food. They can open their mouth wide, and that's curtains for any nearby prey. They eat about anything they can fit in that large mouth—lizards, little mammals, small fish, snails, and insects. Bullfrogs live seven to ten years. When stressed, afraid, or trying to fend off a predator, and that may be a human, they will pee on you with the hopes you drop them.

Grudges can be deep and loud, at least in your head, as you replay how you were wronged, hurt, and shamed. With a grudge it's like one opens their large mouth to "catch" negative about the wrongdoer. This makes the person feel in charge, and they will judge and gossip to try and achieve that. It's more like their insecurity. Bullfrogs are voracious eaters, and gossip and rumors can be insatiable, ruining relationships and reputations. The victim in the fallout can end up depressed and anxious and in such despair that they could have suicidal ideation. With the spreading of rumors, nobody seems to look for the truth. Like the life span of a bullfrog, grudges can, unfortunately, live for years and affect many others. Frogs can carry viruses, bacteria, fungi, and parasites, as well as secrete toxins from their skin. So don't risk being peed on. Let's leave the bullfrogs to their own pond, and we stay in our healthy pond.

Skills to try:

1. Examine if you are holding any grudges. Understand why it is wrong to do so. Stop any gossip or rumors. Rumors are spread and usually run their course, whereas gossip involves a personal or scandalous detail. It usually causes a significant amount of hurt and humiliation.

2. Seek to understand what happened. Listen to another's side of the story.

3. Accept what happened. Life does happen, good and bad. Determine if you played any role.

Matthew 7:1–2 (NIV), "Do not judge, or you too will be judged. For in the same way you judge others; you will be judged, and with the measure you use, it will measured to you."

We are not to judge or hold grudges. We can only judge if we do so without being a hypocrite, without giving a negative evaluation, if we don't pronounce guilt, and if we don't criticize. Only God knows all that's happening with the other person. We must put away the pointy finger.

Response:

_____

_____

_____

_____

_____

_____

_____

_____

_____

_____

_____

_____

_____

_____

_____

_____

_____

Negative Thinking

Overcoming an Eddy

I was born and raised in Nova Scotia, Canada. In a village where I spent summers, there was a wharf that had eddies. Eddies are circular currents like a whirlpool. I had watched some kids try to jump near the swirling water and was scared that one of them could get caught in the swirl. Well, in case you are wondering what that has to do with anything, here is the comparison. Negative thinking is like an eddy. Get caught in this thinking, and it can suck the life out of you. It will pull you under. It has already become a habit that has made you have less joy and likely have feelings of helplessness. It can make you feel anxious, and it can lead to chronic stress. Don't forget those important brain chemicals you are depleting with your negative thinking.

If you were caught in an eddy, how would you get out? A person has to make aggressive forward strokes to power through. The whirlpool has a grasp, a swirling motion you need to break free from its downward pull. And by comparison don't you feel like negative thinking has pulled you down and you have not been that strong of a person but a person you can hardly recognize—one who is anxious, worried, and sad and has no fun anymore?

A study in the American Academy of Neurology found that negative thinking diminishes your brain's ability to think, reason, and form memories. Essentially draining your brain's resources. In the same journal, it was found that cynical thinking also produces a greater dementia risk.

First, let's look at a Bible character, the apostle Paul. He had many challenges happen to him, such as being shipwrecked three times, robbed, beaten, imprisoned, and stoned. He reports he had perils from his own countrymen, from false brethren, the wilderness, the city, and the sea. He was also weary, cold, hungry, naked, persecuted, and had a thorn in his flesh. While in prison he was abandoned by his friends. He despaired of life. How did he get through those "whirlpools of life"? He pulled through life by the power of the Holy Spirit working in and through and for him. You have to forge your path through with skills to counteract the habit of negativity.

Paul also knew that no matter what circumstance he found himself in, he should give thanks. When we express gratitude, our brain releases the hormones that make us feel happier. Gratitude helps a person deal with adversity and improve their health and relationships. It reduces stress and helps one be more resilient. It is also hard to stay in a self-pity mood if expressing gratefulness.

The pessimistic side of negative thinking, where our pessimistic mind wants to go most of the time, is not always accurate. That voice can be called a critical voice, and it will drive you bananas even though, for the most part, it is meant to keep you safe. An example is, "I should go; no, I shouldn't go; well, if I go, I will not be okay." Then you might feel anxious and experience your blood pressure going up. You know, there was no threat to going to that person's house, but your brain was not in logic mode. If you are thinking a lot in "I shoulds," you are putting guilt on yourself with added pressure. Instead, tell yourself, "I am having an anxious thought right now; I will choose to think this through without the drama of anxiety." Or say, "I will come up with a better way to self-manage."

I have a niece who has a gratitude journal. She reports, "It helps a lot on rough days to be reminded of the good things that have happened since time goes by, and it can be forgotten." She adds, "In our house, everyone is required to say something positive or what they are grateful for if they said something negative or are having a grumpy day." Also, "Repeats are not allowed; it has to be different each time." My niece reports this practice has really worked. Bravo, family!

Skills to try:

1. Get out of your head, where you go over and over again over your experiences that did not work out and where you do not feel happy. Stop the merry-go-round thinking!

2. Do not personalize where you believe you are at fault for all life going wrong. Take responsibility only for your part.

3. Keep track of your thoughts for a day, and when you have a negative thought, replace it with a positive thought. This takes practice, so have patience.

4. Like one caught in a whirlpool, keep moving forward with necessary changes.

5. Begin a gratitude journal. It will boost your mood. It helps a person keep track of where life is good when there are challenges. Write three things in the morning and three in the evening that you are grateful for and repeat the next day and so on. In one month you will have 180 expressions of thankfulness. You will be so busy

giving thanks that it will help dispel the negativity.

Second Corinthians 12:9 (NIV), "But He [the Lord] said to me. 'My grace is sufficient for you, for my power is made perfect in weakness.'"

God can take our weaknesses or liabilities and use them to demonstrate His power. He surrounds us with His grace, and that is enough. He is always more than enough.

Response to skills:

_____

_____

_____

_____

_____

_____

_____

_____

_____

_____

_____

_____

_____

_____

Negative Thinking Is Like
Not Pulling Your Weeds

On the previous pages, I compared negative thinking to being in an eddy that can pull you under. Now I compare it to not pulling your weeds. When I walk by my flower bed and see some weeds and leave them there, then the next time I pass by and there are more, it is like negative thinking. It gets out of hand. If I allow myself to think negative thoughts, I become my own worst enemy, and the thinking seems to have a bad influence on almost every part of my life. It squeezes out the positive. I can't see the flowers, fruit, or vegetables because the negative thinking (weeds) has choked them out.

It goes like this, "What I think affects how I feel, and how I feel I act out." For example, if you have allowed your brain to be in "I can't mode," "I will never get out of this situation," or "I am a failure," then it may become more obvious why depression is hanging around. Depression creates negative thinking, and negative thinking creates depression.

Some weeds are poisonous; some are very persistent; others will sting, and some will get out of control. And there are those that cause allergies/hay fever. There are many reasons people are negative thinkers other than maybe depression has set in. Consider if you are a worrier, pessimistic, oversensitive, a complainer, or stay in the fight-or-flight response, so you have too much of that cortisol filling up your brain. Negative thinkers mostly think they are not good enough, not attractive enough, not athletic enough, or not smart enough.

There is a Bible character named Gideon. Gideon had a hard time with his negative thinking. He was rather a coward and had an inferiority complex. He said his family was poor, and he was the least in his father's house. Gideon saw himself as unfit for God's service. God uses our weakness to cause us to depend on Him (Judges 6–8).

We are rather like that at times: doubters. An angel greeted Gideon with "mighty warrior." Was that a sense of humor from an angel? Maybe we don't realize that God sees us being warriors. He sees us as a finished product, capable men and women in His hands when we follow His leading. God was quite patient with Gideon, and we have needed a lot of patience as well. He was also weak in faith. Again, many of us were also.

Skills to try:

1. Attend to your garden by pulling all your weeds (negative thinking). You can't leave a root. It grows back, and the root system underneath could be vast.

2. List your strengths and what you like about yourself in these areas—spiritually, physically, emotionally, socially, and mentally—and add your abilities. Maybe you can ask others who know you well for added input. This skill will counteract your negative thinking.

3. Stop comparing yourself to others. This is so damaging to your psyche. If you get back in the mode of "others have; others do, and I can't," then recheck for negative thinking roots.

4. Look at my page on "Evict the Bad Guest." You are looking for negative thinking or cognitive distortions. It probably is causing you to lack motivation and have depression and anxiety. Monitor what you are thinking in comparison to your mood, and you will see the connection.

Judges 8:23 (NIV), "But Gideon told them [the Israelites], 'I will not rule over you, nor will my son rule over you. The Lord will rule over you.'"

So we have Gideon as a fearful and doubtful man, definitely not up to the challenge God gave him, and he ended up becoming a hero. Seems like God looks at what we can become.

Response:

_____

_____

_____

_____

_____

_____

_____

_____

_____

_____

_____

_____

_____

_____

_____

_____

_____

The Wasp and the Caterpillar

Consider this strong statement, "Some wasp species inject a parasite into a caterpillar, and that developing larvae will cause the caterpillar to grow weak and die." This comparison is about negative thinking. It is like your parasite. It will weaken everything in your life. No need to list the bad effects as you know them; you experience them. It is time to detoxify your system!

What caused this negative thinking? It can come from medical issues, life events, certain personalities like pessimism, insecurity, or even substance abuse. The amygdala in the brain has a tendency to remember and give credence to negative experiences more than positive ones. Triggers and any current mental health concerns have to be considered as well. Self-esteem and environment may come into play as determining factors, as negative thinkers usually feel insecure and have false beliefs about themselves and the world.

One of the ways negative thinking shows up is in an attitude of being cynical. That means you don't trust people and their motives. They are unpleasant, contemptuous, or pessimistic. This happens when people feel hurt or angry about something, so it is a defense against being hurt and discouraged again. This person believes that cynical thinking is a way to protect themself from things that are out of control. It is a belief that humans do what they do because they are selfish and the world is bad. This person had hopes, but they were dashed, so thinking and expressing their negativity can come across as being Grumbly Garrett, who holds grudges and keeps a scorecard against you, making it hard to have a friendship with him.

234

Here is a list to see how bad you might be in the negative thinking "habit." Do you blame yourself for negative circumstances, but there is no evidence to validate it? Do you have tendencies to beat yourself up on a regular basis? Do you have a hard time finding any positives in your life? Do you turn one negative event into the snowball effect, making it bigger and bigger as it rolls along? Do you jump to conclusions too regularly? Are you generally a pessimist about the future? Do you take issues that have nothing to do with you and make them about you? How many of the seven questions did you answer yes? Well, let's get to solutions.

Skills to try:

1. Ask yourself what is causing you to feel and respond in a negative way.

2. Is there anything that is holding you back from letting the negative feeling or thinking go? You actually have a choice to let go and get back to important living.

3. Can the situation be changed, or do you just need to develop more coping skills?

4. Try to look at each situation from every perspective. Can it be reframed? For example, instead of thinking you can't do something or go somewhere, change what you say to yourself by saying, "There is no danger there, and I can get in the car and try."

5. Instead of berating yourself for your negative self-talk, be your "bestie." What would Beverly Bestie tell you about your concern? Remember she is encouraging and helpful.

6. If you like journaling your negative thoughts, then every place you had a negative thought or feeling, tell yourself you are breaking up with "Negative Newton" or "Negative Nora" and replace it with a positive feeling or thought. How about replacing it with Positive Penelope or Optimistic Otto?

235

7. Try meditation/prayer. It will help with self-awareness and detaching yourself from your thoughts and emotions. Prayer connects to the best resource, who gives the perfect response.

8. Stop blaming. It takes two to tango. Take responsibility.

9. Press the stop button on the tape where you go over and over again over your errors.

10. Control your attitude. If it stinks, make it smell good. Try and find what is causing the bad attitude. Maybe it is work, family, finances, or a bad conversation with a friend. Once you find out what is bothering you, then you can do something about it.

11. To stop cynical thinking, you have to first admit you are cynical. Then work to learn to be positive. Attempt to give authentic compliments to other people and do something nice for somebody else. This is an area that is difficult, as compliments come across as backhanded. Practice gratitude. Find the root cause of your cynical thinking. Probably you will find someone hurt you, in which case a mental health professional can assist. It will also help if you keep company with positive people, as you can learn from their worthwhile people skills.

Philippians 4:8 (NIV), "Finally, brothers…whatever is true, whatever is noble, whatever is right, whatever is pure, whatever is lovely, whatever is admirable, if anything is excellent or praiseworthy—think about such things."

Do not fill your mind and heart with the things of the world. We are what we think.

Setting your mind on the positive brings us to wholeness.

Response:

_____

_____

_____

_____

_____

_____

_____

_____

_____

_____

_____

_____

_____

_____

_____

_____

_____

_____

_____

_____

Courage and Self-Confidence

You Are Braver than You Believe

Christopher Robin told Winnie the Pooh the following quote:

"You are braver than you believe, stronger than you seem, and smarter than you think."

In this quote Christopher Robin tries to tell Pooh that he is going to be gone for a while. Pooh says he is quite lost and not strong enough without him and nobody will be there to give him wisdom. Christopher Robin reassures Pooh, "Even when we're apart, I will always be with you." Haven't we all felt helpless at times? Haven't we all felt not as strong as we wanted or needed to be? Haven't we had times we needed the wisdom from our special discerning friends and family? That has been me, for sure. But look at the insight and love of Christopher Robin, "I will always be with you." That sounds like a great friendship, but it resonates with the character of the Lord as well—He will always be with us.

A brave person is a person who sees a dangerous situation and immediately reacts bravely without thinking. Courage is seeing a situation, a dangerous or scary experience, and acting in spite of one's fear. As a mental health concern, I am addressing this because the opposite of courage is fear. If you have anxiety, courage is quite important, and the fear will only make things worse. Courage is the antidote. Courage will also build confidence and cause you to believe in yourself. Having courage will show up in all areas of your life. You will feel like you can take a risk, that you have power, as well as you mastered your emotions.

Most of us agree that first responders are the standard for showing courage. As we give thanks to those who run into burning buildings and forests, who put their lives in danger to keep the public safe, the tireless efforts of medical personnel to care for the ill and injured, and the military who fight for our freedom, consider these examples that you may not think are actually courageous.

Envision those who get up daily to face the task of taking care of their loved one who has a medical or progressive neurodegenerative condition or a mental illness. Some choose to face living with someone who has been abusive or has wronged them in other ways and altered their life forever. Quite a few carry on despite living with a disability that is very difficult for their existence personally and in living in society. It takes fortitude for the lonely to make attempts to overcome their emptiness. There are people who are going through various stages of grief and persevere in spite of the pain. I admire those who have had a very rough childhood and display courage to learn ways to be an overcomer. Some environments are so rough that it is safer to live on the streets than at home. Many have the daunting task of facing chemotherapy, surgery, or even their fear of going to a dentist even though their care is by professionals. Quite a number live in poverty, but they keep trying to improve their lives and the lives of their children in spite of the odds.

There are those who are imprisoned, unaccounted for as POWs, in the military, on the mission field, or on other assignments and the challenges of that and their families, who may be struggling due to those situations. Some experience a workplace that does not treat them as they deserve, and others struggle in their hunt for work daily to sustain their family. There is an increasing number of grandparents who made a choice to raise their grandchildren in spite of aging and their own health. Fostering and adopting may not be easy endeavors.

Other gutsy aspects are going on a job interview, performing on stage or in sports, doing public speaking, or standing up to a bully. It takes fortitude to ask for help when needed. It takes tenacity to admit when you are wrong, take responsibility, say no when necessary, and do a new or risky thing. It takes determination to face rejection and ridicule. It is challenging to move to a new locale and start at a new school or employment. It takes gumption to say hello for the first time and goodbye for the last time. To be courageous does not mean you don't have fear.

I am giving highlights and don't want to miss your valiant efforts at what you deal with on a regular basis. Due to space, for now, I acknowledge the determination, strength, endurance, and danger of those who face the challenges. Kudos to all my fellow human beings as you face what you must today. May God be with you. Keep hope.

Skills to try:

1. I can understand that with those trials comes exhaustion and feeling overwhelmed. Don't take it flippantly that I am saying to care for yourself first. Caregivers and those in the helper or service fields can easily get burnout. Oftentimes they try to do more than they are able.

2. Know when to walk away from an argument or fight or even to stand alone. Call in resources if needed.

3. If your relationship is toxic, then wisely consider your sanity and leave it. Counsel with trusted people is recommended.

4. Turn toward a situation or trigger that causes you to fear and act rather than be in avoidance. It will empower you. My personal example is my mom raised me to take music lessons. I chose the guitar, and after the second lesson, my teacher said I had to be in a recital. I refused, as I was too new and figured I would embarrass myself. I wonder what would have happened if I had stuck with it and faced the fear.

5. Be willing to be vulnerable, ask for help if necessary, get feedback and admit when wrong.

6. Take a stand against things that are wrong, such as racism, bullying, disrespect, or abuse.

7. Manage disappointment while trying to succeed; see it as temporary and keep hope.

Psalm 112:7 (NIV), "[He] will have no fear of bad news; [his] heart is steadfast, trusting in the Lord."

We have assurance twenty-four seven that we do not need to fear anything. God is aware of all things that concern us, and we have His presence. We live, so we will receive bad news, but God holds our life, our future, in His loving and trustworthy hands. "To be steadfast" means "to be firm, determined, unyielding, and faithful."

Response:

_____

_____

_____

_____

_____

_____

_____

_____

_____

_____

_____

_____

_____

_____

_____

_____

_____

_____

_____

_____

_____

Quite the Mother

There are so many wonderful examples of people who have shown courage, and we all will have a different perspective on this. I admire Nelson Mandela, who fought against apartheid (racial oppression), and Harriett Tubman, who overcame her disability (a head injury) and helped lead slaves to freedom on an underground railroad. For today, there was a woman named Mother Teresa, and I feel sure you will like her story and her struggle. It is definitely a tale of courage.

Mother Teresa was born as Agnes Bojaxhiu in 1910. She was a great humanitarian who devoted her entire life to helping the sick and poor. When she was eight years old, her father died, and Agnes became very close to her mother, Drana. Drana was deeply committed to charity work and instilled in her daughter a love for the destitute. Drana regularly invited the hungry to dine with them. Her mom also taught her to not eat a single bit unless she had shared the food with others. Her calling to devote her life to Christ came at age twelve. At age eighteen Agnes decided to become a nun and was given the name Sister Mary Teresa. Her first assignment as a nun was at a girls' school in Calcutta, India, where she dedicated herself to alleviating girls' poverty through education. Her prayer on behalf of the girls was, "Give me the strength to be ever the light of their lives so that I may lead them at last to you."

Another call came to Sister Teresa at the age of thirty-six to establish a hospice, centers for the blind, aged, and disabled, and those with leprosy. She left her convent and, after six months of medical training, then ventured into the slums of Calcutta with a goal of aiding "the unwanted, the unloved, and the uncared for." She became Mother Teresa when she made her final vows to a life of poverty, chastity, and obedience. I can only imagine the intensity of this call.

Mother Teresa wanted the people of Calcutta to have something tangible, so she started an open-air school. As donations came in, a leper colony, orphanage, nursing home, a family clinic, and several mobile health clinics were established. Then onto New York in 1971, where she opened a house of charity, and in 1985, she started a home for those infected with HIV/AIDS. By the time of her death in 1997, at age eighty-seven, she had started six hundred and ten foundations in one hundred and twenty-three countries around the world (Biography Newsletter, April 27, 2017). That is nearly seventy years of helping the impoverished. Reaching others in a place like Calcutta, where there is a seventy percent poverty rate, shows something beyond courage. Mother Teresa said, "It is not how much we give but how much love we put into giving."

There is a story in Mark 12:41–44 and Luke 21:2–3 about a poor widow who gave two very small coins, called mites, to the temple treasury. The account of the story is that the rich gave out of their wealth, but she gave out of her poverty, giving everything she had to live on. Mother Teresa gave tirelessly because she loved the Lord and the people. The widow in the story gave her all because she loved the Lord. What she had left was unknown. It takes courage and faith to carry on without any knowledge of what tomorrow holds. We can take courage in what we are called to do by exercising faith and doing the work of His service from a standpoint of love. God looks at the sacrifice.

"By blood, I am Albanian, by citizenship an Indian, by faith, I am a Catholic nun. As to my calling, I belong to the world. As to my heart I belong entirely to the heart of Jesus" (Mother Teresa).

Skills to try:

1. Do not live by fears, insecurities, or the negative opinion of others. Seek the One who has the perfect opinion of you and the right direction for your life. That in itself takes courage—to go against what others do and think.

2. Be vulnerable, especially when it will help others.

3. Nurture the strength within you. Develop resilience and trust and know and express your values, as you will need courage to stick with your principles. Be careful of compromising.

4. Be conscious of how your actions affect others. Be sure you display right from wrong.

5. Inspire others by your example and your leadership.

6. Do not worry about things you have no control over.

7. Mother Teresa started a multitude of new things. Don't be afraid to get started and be innovative. With that comes the risk of failure. Therefore, if failure happens, treat it as a learning experience.

8. Do you have a "mite" you can use to get you started in something even if you don't know the outcome? Do you desire to give a "mite" for a cause that you feel passionate about? Maybe start by volunteering to get some insight.

Second Corinthians 9:7 (NIV), "Every man should give what he has decided in his heart to give, not reluctantly or under compulsion, for God loves a cheerful giver."

Catch the two words "not reluctantly." We are to serve and give eagerly. Keep in mind courage comes in many forms—physical, emotional, intellectual, social, moral, or spiritual. Courage, trust, and faith are good triplets to be friends with.

Response:

_____

_____

_____

_____

_____

_____

_____

_____

_____

_____

_____

_____

_____

_____

_____

_____

_____

_____

_____

_____

Loneliness

Leah's Story

Three out of five Americans are lonely. It seems like nobody is immune. Being alone and loneliness are not the same thing. Being alone has to do with how much your relationships meet your needs and whether or not your life is satisfying, whereas loneliness is about your relationships not being where they should be, and there is dissatisfaction. AARP conducted a survey in 2018 that reported 31 percent of married people forty-five years of age and older felt lonely.

What is it about married people feeling lonely? There are several reasons, such as the spouse or partner do not talk enough to each other, there are disappointments, lack of emotional intimacy, and general unhappiness with family life. There can be work pressures, general stress, and even unrealistic expectations. There are parental responsibilities, lack of energy, and possible priorities that changed.

When there is an emotional chasm between two in the married relationship, it could be also because they lost intentional connection time to talk over the day and events. They grew apart and stopped offering hugs, kisses, pats, and feels on body parts.

They stopped giving the "come-hither glances" and stopped compliments. Meals were eaten with little conversation or in separate places, and outside activities like theatre, concerts, walks, and dinners were stopped. Fun seemed to end. Married life became mundane.

In Genesis 29 in the Bible, there were two sisters, Leah and Rachel, married to the same man, Jacob. Leah was not loved by her husband, but Rachel was very much loved. Leah was able to give her husband seven children in hopes she would be loved. "This time my husband will treat me with honor" (Genesis 30:20, NIV). I don't think that happened. Leah was lonely. It seems like all she got were visits with hopes of getting pregnant. She was not validated or appreciated but rather just tolerated. It is quite sad. Be careful that your relationship does not slip into this. Protect the nest (your home and life there) and the birdies in it. By the way, birds who build nests are very resourceful. They will use about anything to accomplish the build.

My husband and I are early risers, so it's easy to have coffee and tea together and any conversation. We make it a priority. That is a big key to prioritizing each other. This may include prayer time. Especially on Sunday I try and tell him how nice he looks in his shirt and tie, and he tells me about my pretty attire. I also give him thanks for shopping and for the many meals he makes. He is told he is appreciated for helping with the housework. He is better at it than I am. When we had to isolate due to my being sick, he let me know he missed me and our time together. I liked that. It is that simple to stay connected.

Skills to try:

1. Talk to each other to find out where your marriage got off track. Start problem-solving to regain focus on each

other again. Be affirming, supportive, attentive, and recommit to each other to work through the issues. Be a good listener. Tell each other what the positive things are to balance out where the challenges are. See if you can make that conversation stress-reducing. You will get further with marital repair if you don't add judging and blaming. Be sure to take responsibility for yourself. Examine if there is a difference in perception, such as household responsibilities or finances. Tell each other what you need and want. This can be surprising, as it could be something as simple as a date every other week or help with the housework and kids. Remember special days. Seek counseling if needed. This is not my marriage counseling but suggestions.

2. Notice, notice, notice! Your partner is not a mind reader. As you are making attempts to reconnect with each other, give compliments and express gratitude for small and large things and everything in between. If the house is nicely picked up and the meal was delicious, then say so. How about a thanks for the yard getting mowed so regularly? What about, "Honey, I noticed you got all the errands done; thanks so much"? If things look like the day was challenging, ask what you can do to be helpful. Be the first to give a good word to your spouse before they head out the door to work, as somebody of the opposite sex could beat you to it. That's a different subject.

3. Beating loneliness and a humdrum relationship includes not expecting your spouse or partner to be your entire world. Be sure to communicate always with your spouse or partner, but have other friends and family to enjoy time with. Make sure they are friends that share your values and morals. Do not allow this time to be full of complaints against your partner. How can a person recover a potential relationship with your friends if they are being bad-mouthed?

4. What are the creative and resourceful ways to build or rebuild your nest?

Psalm 31:24 (NIV), "Be strong and take heart, all you who hope in the Lord."

"To take heart" is "to have confidence in something and have courage." Leah didn't have much of a chance of finding favor with her husband. However, we never lose when we keep hoping no matter the distresses of life.

Response:

_____

_____

_____

_____

_____

_____

_____

_____

_____

_____

_____

_____

_____

It's Kind of Like a Beast

"People think I'm odd, so I know how it feels to be different, and I know how lonely that can be." This is a quote from the Disney movie *Beauty and the Beast.*

Feeling lonely can feel like a beast, and one may be lonely because they feel different. Different can be described as feeling like an outsider or not fitting in. Loneliness can be debilitating, with a side of emptiness and worthlessness as well as downright hurting. It hurts because loneliness acts on the same part of the brain as physical pain. It also means that one's current relationships do not meet their needs or there are no relationships. Loneliness is a major risk factor for increasing depression and anxiety. When lonely, the stress hormone cortisol increases, which compromises one's immune system and causes cognitive decline, and several medical conditions can result. It can lead to early death.

The animator for the Beast decided to draw him as a twenty-one-year-old who is insecure, wants to be loved, wants to love, but has this ugly exterior he needs to overcome. That exterior is a mixture of several animals. Well, God made us to be social beings and need each other and love each other. We also are a "mixture" in many ways, such as looks, personality, nationality, culture, etcetera.

There is a myriad of things that can cause loneliness. The lonely person may feel unworthy, defeated, insecure, or unimportant. Some may be self-conscious or have self-esteem issues. Possibly people have been disappointing to them, or their childhood family was "different." Some who are experiencing loneliness have a history of being bullied, and others may be part of being LGBTQ and dealing with acceptance. Other factors are one's location, job assignment, transportation issues, personal mobility or hearing or sight issues, and recent life changes such as moving, death of a loved one, or divorce. If one is a caretaker to another person, one may not be able to reach out beyond that responsibility. Those in the military experience a lot of loneliness, and so do their families. Incarcerated individuals may feel lonely, as well as those connected to them. Finances, aging concerns, and being in assisted living are big factors as well.

Some lonely people's approach to others is one in which they may be defensive. When in some social situations, they just do not find the connections enjoyable, possibly due to personal awkwardness or feeling that people are judging them and ready to reject them. Others just lack coping skills. Social media is both positive and negative, as it is a connection but not face to face, where physical touch can happen and endorphins are more likely to occur. Empty nesters and even those in midlife experience changes, as adjustments are not always easy, and important parent-child connections have moved out. Some parents look forward to the empty nest, but I was the opposite. When my last child moved out to college, I was a sad camper, as he was a bright spot to my day and very easy to be around.

If you are good with loneliness, then let it be so. My experience says that most people don't like it and the holidays are especially hard on them. For those who want to take a chance and move out from how it feels emotionally dismal, then try these skills:

Skills to try:

1. Make a deliberate attempt to make a connection by phone, text, email, or, better yet, in person. Try walking or going to a dog park. Try making the first move. Make a suggestion to have lunch or drinks. My X neighbor

gentleman met once a week with other men for donuts and coffee.

2. Get out in nature. Get a zoo membership. Join a club or take a class of which you have an interest. Do a home improvement project. Help others with their project.

3. Volunteer. It feels good to help others or animals, and it is good for your community. It will boost your self-esteem and fuel your pride. It will give you a sense of purpose.

4. Talk to acquaintances, neighbors, and people you have not met. I walk my dog around the neighborhood and have met six strangers who I now consider friends.

5. Plan ahead. If you know you will be alone for a holiday or an extended time, then know how you will organize your day and weeks. My mother used to be sure she had a few puzzles and books around and would go to a movie, day bus trip, or an auction.

6. Watch out for those negative expressions, such as "nobody cares" or "life is not fair." Counteract those thoughts. Tell yourself that people do care but are busy or away for now and that life is fair but has challenges. Tell yourself that you can problem-solve them and learn from them.

7. Make a present for yourself or for someone who has a birthday or for Christmas. The internet is full of ideas, and you may find yourself developing a fun new hobby. I want to try pottery, and I already do scrapbooking. I might even start taking care of a young plant and keep it going for a few weeks, then give it as a gift. A favorite gift I received was a homemade candle.

Deuteronomy 31:8 (NIV), "The Lord Himself goes before you and will be with you; He will never leave you nor forsake you. Do not be afraid; do not be discouraged."

"The Lord Himself" will be with us. Moses is commissioning

Joshua, but we have the Holy Spirit always. Therefore, we need not be afraid or discouraged. It's a promise. Hold onto it.

Response:

_____

_____

_____

_____

_____

_____

_____

_____

_____

_____

_____

_____

_____

_____

_____

It's All about Who Wore the Robe

Have you ever wondered about the woman in the Bible who had the issue of blood for twelve years? That is about four thousand, three hundred and eighty days of dealing with that malady. It may have been painful and certainly draining as estrogen levels peak and fall. In those days the woman was considered unclean, and anything she touched, sat on, or lay on was considered unclean. This unnamed woman—Jesus called her daughter—was suffering. She lived in isolation like a castaway because of her condition, and for that number of years, her presence in any public place would have been frowned on. That is a lot of segregation and sadness (Mark 5:24–34, Matthew 9:20–22, and Luke 8:43–48).

I picked this unfortunate soul to talk about loneliness because imagine nobody can be around you and hasn't been for twelve years. She was quarantined. You know how most of us had cabin fever with our quarantine for COVID. There was no cure for her; she was doomed to stay that way unless some miracle happened. She heard about Jesus and, in her desperation, pressed through a crowd that probably disparaged her. She touched the hem of His robe and was instantly healed.

What about you? Are you desperate for a change, whatever that may be? Could it be work-life balance, a health concern, getting rid of toxic relationships, saving for something important, more time to get out with positive friends and family, or improving your spiritual condition? The woman was healed by touching the Master's robe. She did not reach to touch His body because she was unclean and forbidden by law to even be out there. She was going to touch something on Him. It was not about the robe but who wore the robe. Immediately Jesus perceived that power went out from Him

(Luke 8:46). Did you ever wonder why Jesus asked, "Who touched Me?" After all, He knows everything. Maybe He wanted her to be seen publicly as someone who experienced a miracle and could return to living with her family and be in society again and had faith. Isn't that with us as well to return to healthy, happy living, not so full of depression, anxiety, worry, and fear, and return to Christ more fully and have faith in Him for what we need?

She needed mercy big time, and she got it. She was very intentional. This is what may be missing for those lonely people who don't try hard enough to get out and move from isolation to making friends. Of course, there could be mobility concerns with those who have medical issues. Although I understand that introverts often do prefer to be alone rather than in a crowd, there is something to be said about the value of friendships as an antidote for loneliness. By the way, being an introvert is a personality trait, not a disorder. Solitude can be healthy, as one can recharge. However, if you don't give it a good intentional try, too much isolation can be problematic and lead to depression.

There has been a stigma about introverted people that they don't try hard enough to overcome being alone. This is unfair of society. Some reasons for this are they may feel vulnerable, insecure, anxious, and don't feel like they have "enough" to offer for social interaction. Somewhere along the line, self-esteem took a hit, and being home alone or with one or two became more comfortable. Maybe they are happy being alone. Those with social anxiety fall into this category. Albert Einstein was an introvert, and Bill Gates is said to be as well. So, introverts, you are okay, but if you want to reach out more, read the skills below.

Skills to try:

1. Don't be something you are not. For sure, let go of any shame. It is okay to go alone and be alone. Solitude can be good; isolation, not so good.

2. Do not be afraid if there is any rejection. You are so much more than another person's opinion. Go and make friends. Work on not being shy. Take a risk. Know your worth.

3. Volunteer. Take it slow, but be patient and intentional. It takes a while to get motivated and build confidence, but don't stand still. Make goals.

4. It is okay to take time before you speak; a good quality is to think things through first, but do speak up and be heard and get to know others and let yourself be known.

5. Set boundaries and control your environment. If you need downtime, then take it. Have a wingman or wing woman if you expect it will be too difficult. Practice anti-anxiety skills.

6. The woman who was suffering was desperate, so she reached for her miracle. Be desperate about changing anything holding you back from living life to the fullest. Reach for your answer.

Romans 8:31a (NIV), "If God be for us, who can be against us?"

God is for us all who are in Christ. No matter what, Christ has us. It is our privilege and blessing.

Response:

_____

_____

_____

_____

_____

_____

_____

_____

_____

_____

_____

_____

_____

_____

_____

_____

_____

_____

_____

Regrets

The Game of Snakes and Ladders Is Like Regrets

In my younger years, I played a game called Snakes and Ladders. When you move your game piece to a square with a ladder, you advance up, and when you come to a snake, you slither down. That is like regret. Keeping regrets is like the snake in which you go down (depression), and going up the ladder is a way you move past it.

"Regret" is defined "as sorrow or disappointment over something that a person did or didn't do, such as a missed opportunity or a loss." If you obsess over your regrets, you will likely find yourself falling into depression. Regrets can last moments, days, weeks, months, or years. It's those years of regrets, especially, that haunt you and can have damaging effects on your mind and body. It is hard to escape from when you think too much on what your perceived better choice was and how you did or didn't take it or do it.

In the Bible Judas Iscariot betrayed Jesus for thirty pieces of silver. His regrets were so tremendous that he threw the money in the temple and went out and hung himself. Do not let any regrets lead you to self-destruction!

My regrets lasted for years. I regretted selling a condo and regretted not being further along spiritually or financially. I regretted some things I said to others that were uncalled for, which is rare for me, as I am very kind. It caused me significant insomnia and sadness. I regret that I couldn't do more for my children, such as pay for college.

It is the "biggie" regrets that plague people the most, such as infidelity, abortions, addictions, crimes, divorce, choosing work over family, not graduating, not taking care of one's health, and not burying the hatchet. People often regret not having courage or confidence and not listening to God.

Not listening to God indicates you may be too independent. People are so busy, and they don't take the time to get quiet and listen to His still, small voice. Individuals generally do not like being vulnerable, so they skip coming to God with their troubles of yesterday and today. However, being vulnerable and trusting our supreme being is where a person will make a connection with God and satisfy their deep longings. After all, He knows all about us. He also speaks through His Word, which means we need to read it.

Start each day as if you woke up with a clean slate. Picture this. Do not bring the mistakes of your past still written on your new clean slate of a new day. The *Merriam-Webster Dictionary* defines a "clean slate" as "a person's record that shows no evidence of any problems, broken rules, etcetera." A good exercise to do is to literally get an eraser and tell God you are giving Him your past and start erasing. An eraser from any dollar store or using a paper towel will work and serve as a reminder to be wary to not repeat those mistakes again.

In the judicial system, misdemeanor cases can be sealed after a period of time has passed without any more convictions. It starts by getting a certificate of eligibility; then, if your state approves that, a person will petition for relief. The judge gets the final say. What does this have to do with anything? God is the ultimate judge. He makes you eligible to have your past record of mistakes sealed if you ask for forgiveness. He also will give you relief from your regrets because He knows best how to bring healing from distraught emotions. Sounds like we, the defendants, should take this best offer.

"If you think you have blown God's plan for your life, rest in this: You, my beautiful friend are not that powerful" (Lisa Bever).

Skills to try:

1. Can you learn from your regrets? The alternative may be staying stuck, self-hate, or depression. It will suck the life out of you if you let it, and you will have trouble moving forward.

2. Understand yourself and your regret and give it meaning.

3. See regret as an opportunity to do things differently next time.

4. If you hurt others, do what you can to make amends.

5. Accept yourself. You are human. You can get things wrong but improve future decisions.

6. Get support with family and friends. Others may have a perspective you can learn from.

7. Ask God to forgive you. Forgive yourself. Let the past be behind you once and for all.

Philippians 3:13 (NIV), "Brothers...I do not consider myself yet to have taken hold of it. But one thing I do: forgetting what is behind and pressing toward what is ahead."

Leaving the past behind, including all the mistakes and regrets, is hard to do. Do not let it rob you of the freedom you can feel when you leave the junk and enjoy tomorrow and what it holds.

Response:

_____

_____

_____

_____

_____

_____

_____

_____

_____

_____

_____

_____

_____

_____

_____

_____

Moving Past the "Biggie" Regrets

On the previous pages, there was a list of a dozen things that people commonly regret. In case you wonder why this is included in a mental health book, it is because people can really struggle to move forward if they feel stuck and sad from their regrets. Oftentimes chronic stress is a result. Add a bit of depression, anxiety, guilt, shame, and helplessness to that mix, and you have a thick "curdled custard of contriteness." If one is ruminating about what they did or didn't do, they are focusing so much on their "error" that it becomes obsessive and can make things worse. Now there is a whole new set of issues, such as looking at their current life with a pessimistic perspective, and all that obsessing can add some medical concerns, such as increased blood pressure, weakened immune system, and insomnia. Even if the person with regrets makes attempts to get back to enjoying life, the regret is never too far from their mind.

By the way, curdled custard can be rescued. Take the split off the heat, put the pan in cold water, and whisk vigorously. Does that remind you that we need to get off the heat (reduce the criticism you have endured) and get into cooler water? Regrets need to be whisked away, but how? Keep reading.

Author Daniel H. Pink reports regrets are in four different categories: foundational, moral, connection, and boldness. He writes that foundational regrets are from not doing the work, such as saving money for retirement, not getting a degree, or not taking care of one's health. Moral regrets are from doing the wrong thing. The example given is bullying or marital infidelity. Connection regrets are of the "if only kind," such as not reaching out to others: family, friends, romantic, and beyond. The fourth is boldness regrets, which is about a chance not taken, such as leaving a dead-end job. You may have played it safe.

Unity, Northeastern Wisconsin's Hospice Provider, reports that the number one regret of terminal patients was that the patient wanted courage to live a life true to themselves, not the life others expected of them. The patients had reported to their nurse, Bonnie Ware, that they looked back and realized they had not fulfilled their dreams. Most of the patients stated it was due to the choices they had made or had not made. It is important to honor as many of your dreams as possible.

In 1 Samuel 24:5–16 David crept up unnoticed and cut off a corner of King Saul's robe. Afterward, David was conscious-stricken. He said to his men, "The Lord forbid that I should do such a thing to my master, the Lord's anointed, or lift my hand against him, for he is the anointed of the Lord" (1 Samuel 24:6, NIV). Is this regret, guilt, shame, remorse, or something else? Before you decide, let's define them. Regret is sorrow, grief, hurt, anger for the pain one feels for oneself, not necessarily for the other person who was hurt. Guilt is a feeling you get that you did something wrong to someone and you acknowledge the harmful action. Shame is the way you view yourself, that you or your life is wrong. It is not related to a specific behavior or event. It makes someone feel like they are bad or inadequate. With remorse there can be moral anguish; you regret the action and take steps to help right the wrong and change.

Right away David felt guilt, as he realized he could have humiliated the king. He may not have liked King Saul, but he had respect for the office of him being king. David's conscience bothered him. David said to King Saul he was not seeking to kill him. David had put his face to the ground and bowed. Saul wept. They parted ways. So what do you say—a case of guilt and remorse?

Skills to try:

1. Acknowledge what you did. Make a sincere apology. Try to communicate with the injured person if possible and be genuine. Have empathy. In the case of David, he explained himself.

2. Make a new set of goals and put one of your dreams on that list. Follow your passion. Don't let fear stop you. Take a look at how to live up to your full potential.

3. Do you need to say "I love you" and other words of endearment more often? Even if you made amends, what about saying "I am sorry" when appropriate?

4. If you are a workaholic and have a tendency to ignore your family, then find balance and give them more time or at least quality time. Don't make excuses for staying at work. When you are at the end of your life, I suspect you will never say, "I spent too much time with my kids." I did many things with my beloved mother, but after she died, I thought of more things I could have done with her just because it made her happy.

5. Picture yourself as a younger man or woman and ask yourself if you did the best you could with the situations you had to face. If you said yes, as you were foolish, immature, had responsibilities put on you, or financial restraints, then forget it and stop beating yourself up. Keep a mindset that always moves forward and seeks to rectify mistakes if possible but then lets them go and move into a lifestyle of recovering your joy.

Romans 12:17 (NIV), "Do not repay anyone evil for evil. Be careful to do what is right in the eyes of everyone."

Do not pay back. Jesus didn't try to get even. It's God's job, and He knows how to do it.

Response:

_____

_____

_____

_____

_____

_____

_____

_____

_____

_____

_____

_____

_____

_____

_____

_____

_____

_____

The Seesaw of Guilt and Shame

A seesaw is a playground piece of equipment for children. It has a fulcrum in the middle and a plank with one end that goes up while the other goes down. That is, to me, a good description of the up-and-down emotions of guilt and shame. Guilt defined is a very strong emotion that arises as a result of an action a person took or did not take. It comes from feeling that one caused another or themselves hurt and pain. Guilt can include feelings of shame, anxiety, frustration, humiliation, and regret. Guilt usually motivates one to change their behavior so they at least do not feel bad. Living with guilt will wear a person down.

Shame is a self-conscious combination of emotions, such as feelings of insecurity, humiliation, anger, embarrassment, worthlessness, powerlessness, inadequacy, suspiciousness, and a general negative belief that there is something wrong with oneself or that they are bad. Shame results when one feels like others are negatively judging them. They feel like they have no value and should be rejected. Shame makes one want to just disappear. Those who feel shame are at risk for depression, anxiety, and loneliness, and they likely are already struggling with low self-esteem. Simply put, guilt is like you made a mistake, and shame is like you are the mistake.

These two heavy planks of guilt and shame cause our lives to go up and down like a seesaw. There could be problems in relating to others. For instance, anger can be a mask to avoid feelings of shame. The anger just diverts attention away from the feelings of shame. Feeling powerless and in despair can come from the real feeling behind it—shame.

If you grew up in a hurtful, disrespectful, or neglect-ful family or you were the target of hostile and abu-sive treatment by peers or adults, then you received some very distorted and perverted messages about the way life is and the way life can be. Shame is the end result of these messages and can quickly lead to acting out your anger in some hurtful and unproduc-tive ways

Dave Decker,
"Shame on You! Understanding
the Shame-Rage Connection,"
The Phoenix Spirit, February 23, 2019

The Bible records an interesting story of a disciple called Peter (John 18:15–27, Matthew 26:31–35, and 69–75) who had denied Christ three times. Peter had such guilt, regret, and shame that he went out and wept bitterly (Luke 22:62). "Bitterly" demonstrates he had severe grief or anguish. As was earlier stated, guilt usual-ly causes one to want to change their behavior. Peter was weak, fearful, and without courage, but he loved the Lord, and his tears were from sincere sorrow for the betrayal. He may have denied Christ, as he feared for his own life. Our feelings cause us to have no control over them at times, but we should be able to control our actions.

The good part of the story is Peter was restored; he turned it around and went and "strengthen his brothers" (Luke 22:32). What's the point? We don't have to stay with those horrible feel-ings of guilt or shame. We can turn it around and even pay forward. Our past is just that, our past. We can start our life again. We are to learn from the past but not dwell there. We are alive, so we will fail. Can we benefit from the seesaw of our tumultuous feelings?

Yes, of course. Peter mended emotionally, was forgiven, and went on to preach to the multitudes.

Skills to try:

1. Name your guilt or shame. For example, "I feel guilty because I hurt your feelings and said bad things about you." You fill in the blank. Accept your feelings. This will help you to feel like it has less power over you. Ask yourself where that feeling came from.

2. If it is a matter of guilt (deserved blame, you did something), can you make it right? Can you commit to change? Can you avoid making the same mistake in the future? Can you apologize? See what you can do to repair the damage. Trust may be lost and may not be able to be regained, but you did your part. Remember everyone makes mistakes.

3. Use "I" statements. An example that happened to me was my husband was not good at giving me my phone messages. I could put him on the defensive and cause a relationship issue, or I could say, "'I feel' discouraged when you don't inform me of who called so I can return the call." I take responsibility for my feelings. It is not "you make me feel annoyed." That could get heated, as we usually have a lot to blame others for. Try this. "I feel" and fill in the blank.

4. Turn negative self-talk into positive self-talk. For example, "I really messed up by not doing my part of the project very well" to "I am human, and I will do better next time."

5. With guilt that comes from a poor choice or action or with shame that perpetuates poor self-esteem, work on it by activities and expressions that boost your self-esteem. Speak out your strengths and what you are good at.

6. Forgive yourself. You will have better feelings of

well-being. Make peace with the past. This will help release the guilt, shame, and resentment. It might keep depression and anxiety at bay.

7. If you have shame, do not allow any victim mentality. There are victims, of course, like in the case of an assault or accident, but to help yourself move past it, do not feel sorry for yourself. It takes patience to heal from what may have been years of injustice. Don't hold anger and resentment. It is a process. Keeping it is like keeping a toxin you might want to use on someone, as well as it is poison to yourself. The world is not against you. God loves you.

8. Help others. That's what the disciple Peter did. He strengthened others. Make a list of how you might be able to do this.

Romans 8:6–7 (NIV), "The mind controlled by the Spirit is life and peace, the sinful mind is hostile to God. It does not submit to God's law, nor can it do so."

It is an awful thought to be hostile to God. Paul was trying to explain that the sinful mind hates the things of God and cannot please God while following the desires of the flesh. The Holy Spirit is our guide, and we must be in tune with Him. Life and peace sound so much better.

Response:

_____

_____

_____

_____

_____

_____

_____

_____

_____

_____

_____

_____

_____

_____

_____

_____

_____

_____

_____

Resilience

The Author, the Rock, and Resilience

I chose this subject of resilience, as we all need it, whether struggling with life, past or present, or with depression and anxiety. There's a host of issues that get thrown at us, and that includes relationship concerns as well. Resilience means the ability to bounce back when things don't go as planned. If someone does not have an ability to be resilient, then they most likely have fallen into depression and frustration with a side of anxiety. Their attitude may very well be "life is wretched."

The beloved author of the Harry Potter series, J. K. Rowling, is a good example to use about resilience. Before she became famous, she was in a "catastrophic marriage," as well as circumstances while in her twenties plunged her into clinical depression. She reported the period of her depression was a time when she had a cold absence of feelings. She was a single mom living on welfare. She was estranged from her father and lost her beloved mother to complications from multiple sclerosis. Ms. Rowling's admission is that at times she felt like she was hanging by a thread. She began to write her novel and was rejected multiple times but did not quit (Oprah Winfrey interview, YouTube, 2015).

"Why this example?" you may be wondering. The way Ms. Rowling coped was she had a strong survival instinct. She added that having been at rock bottom was a solid foundation on which she built her life. There is a part of her journey that has a common denominator for us all. We may have been down, but not out. Many families have estranged relationships. Death happens when we don't want it to and when we still need the one who died. Sometimes we have felt like we hang by a thread during traumatic times. That depression, well, it's very common and seems to take the best of us down a dark hole. I love Ms. Rowling's "do not quit" spirit and her strong survival spirit. I say there is nothing wrong with crying, but then stand strong.

Another great representative of a person who experienced depression and overcame it is "The Rock," Dwayne Johnson. He has shared his story of depression many times. When he was fourteen years old, he and his mom were evicted from their home. Shortly afterward, at age fifteen, his mom attempted suicide in front of him. He saved her by pulling her out of the traffic she walked out in front of. That experience caused him to want to help others. He adds that his depression was severe after his injuries ended his football career. He encourages people to ask for help even if it causes them to feel vulnerable. There are many people I could have used for these examples, but I like who Dwayne is and what he does. It is reported he has twelve charities he supports. He also states that gratitude is his anchor, and joy and hope are the greatest things to give. He adds that attitude and enthusiasm play a big part in his life. He credits his success to self-discipline, dedication, and hard work.

Here are some of The Rock's quotes that have a life lesson:

"If something stands between you and your dream, move it, never be denied."

"When life puts you in tough situations, don't say 'Why me,' just say 'Try me.'"

"You don't need directions, just point yourself to the top and go!"

Skills to try:

1. Can you look at difficult situations as a challenge rather than have the perspective that they will bury you?

2. Can you look at failures and mistakes as lessons to learn from and as opportunities for growth? Resilient people do not allow a difficult circumstance or loss to cause them to give up.

3. Do you feel like you have personal control? Resilient people spend their time and energy focusing on situations that they can get control over.

4. Can you look at the effects of a bad circumstance as temporary rather than permanent?

5. What do you need to do so your survivor spirit will rise up?

Second Corinthians 4:8–9 (NIV), "We are hard pressed on every side, but not crushed: perplexed, but not in despair: persecuted, but not abandoned; struck down, but not destroyed."

Never lose heart. Life may knock you down, but not out. God will come through. Don't quit.

Response:

_____

_____

_____

_____

_____

_____

_____

_____

_____

_____

_____

_____

_____

_____

_____

_____

_____

_____

_____

The Giant Redwood Trees

It is on my bucket list to see the giant redwood trees just because they are magnificent, and I could have a "wow" moment. My love for nature would be mostly satisfied. But there is a comparison to make to further develop a skill for you for resilience.

There is one particular tree called General Sherman amongst the Sequoia redwood trees in California. It is the largest single-stem tree on earth. It tops at 275 feet tall and 25 feet in diameter and is about 2,500 years old. The redwood tree's roots are widespread but somewhat shallow. The roots are interconnected with the roots of other trees where literally they hold each other up. This provides strength against the forces of nature, and they can endure for ages, especially as there is no tap root. The trees grow very close together and are dependent on each other for nutrients as well. It seems that Mother Nature has come up with the team system for strength, support, and sustenance. What a good idea, especially when a person is down and struggling. It is easier to push through when one has someone in their corner "rooting" for them.

Here are some quotes that in themselves are a lesson on resilience.

> *"I can be changed by what happens to me but I refuse to be reduced by it" (Maya Angelou).*
>
> *"Life doesn't get easier or more forgiving, we get stronger and more resilient" (Steve Maraboli).*
>
> *"Courage doesn't always roar, sometimes courage is the quiet voice at the end of the day saying 'I will try again tomorrow'" (Mary Anne Radmacher).*
>
> *"We can learn a lot from trees; they're always*

grounded but never stop reaching heavenward"
(Malay proverb).

Resiliency empowers us to keep on keeping on. It helps one adapt and bounce back. Resilient people, like the redwood trees and their root system of connection, will maintain the right relationships that offer support in trying times. There will always be a death, an illness, a loss of some sort, or a tough challenge, as that is life, and that is rather constant. With resiliency you will be able to draw from your inner strength and rebound from your setbacks. Problems won't go away, but you will be able to move past them, enjoy life more, and better handle stress.

VITAL WorkLife (August 2020) reports that resilient people have five pillars of resilience during tough times. They are awareness, mindfulness, self-care, positive relationships, and purpose.

> *Self-awareness is having a conscious knowledge of your own personality, including strengths, weaknesses, emotions and motivations.*

> *Mindfulness is our ability to be fully present, aware of where we are, what we are doing, and not reactive or overwhelmed by what is going on around us.*

Some may choose to practice meditation or prayer.

> *Self-care is the practice of taking action to maintain or improve our health.*

> *Positive relationships are having those relationships in our lives who support and care for us and we care for them.*

> *Purpose allows us to recognize that we belong or serve something bigger than ourselves.*

Skills to try:

1. Consider "the redwood trees teamwork" of interconnectedness giving support and holding each other up. Let others in. Your crisis is temporary. There are positive people who may have ideas, solutions, or resources that ease the stress.

2. Learn from your mistakes. My niece likes to ask me, "What is God trying to tell you?" I know someone that found a different career when in drug rehab and someone who really didn't need to get a divorce as they did some self-examination.

3. Can you keep calm in the mayhem? Develop skills to keep your peace.

4. Believe in yourself and your ability to succeed.

5. Do something that gives you a sense of achievement. What skills did you use in past struggles that helped you?

6. Take charge. Don't ignore the challenges. What needs to be done? Take action to do it.

7. Like the tree, stay grounded. That means to be emotionally and mentally stable, sensible.

8. Be flexible. That means ready and able to change, adapt to different circumstances easily and calmly, and think quickly.

First Corinthians 16:13 (NIV), "Be on your guard: stand firm in the faith. Be of courage; be strong.

God has a purpose for our lives. To achieve this, we need to stand firm through trials and challenges and have courage. We need to develop resiliency. Ask God to help you with this.

Response:

_____

_____

_____

_____

_____

_____

_____

_____

_____

_____

_____

_____

_____

_____

_____

_____

_____

_____

_____

Helping Children Learn Resiliency

If I asked a dozen people what they think are the most important life skills that children need to learn, they might all have different answers. The common ones would be how to communicate, be empathetic, show respect, have manners, problem-solve, show kindness, and things like how to clean, make healthy choices, make a simple meal, manage money, be punctual, make good decisions, and show gratitude. Of course, there are many more. I am going to talk about resilience because if children don't learn this, then they grow up without much of an ability to deal with life's pressures. They end up having anxiety and other stress-related disorders, such as adjustment disorders or acute stress disorder, to name a few. We all want happier, less stressed kids that can manage through life better than we did. A big part of resilience is being able to deal with one's emotions.

The world the kids are growing up in now is different than the world I grew up in. I would never have disrespected a person in authority, such as a teacher, or let a cuss word out of my mouth, as I knew the consequences. I did not hear about terrorism, but there was war and war protestors. There was no pandemic or being bullied like it is a serious concern now. We did have rebellion, displays of prejudice, the flower children, and a lot of drugs. Families were more nuclear, and there were not as many latchkey kids. There is so much mistrust, doubt, violence, and values that have declined nowadays. The kids can be better prepared for life, which is out of control and full of setbacks, when resiliency skills are taught. They must learn to thrive in spite of confusion abounding and life going haywire.

The American Psychological Association reports these as the top skills needed to build emotional resilience for children:

1. *Self-care*—teach children to not overlook themselves. This includes playing and laughing every day, taking time to be quiet daily, and listening to others.

2. *Socialization*—children learn through face-to-face interactions with others, both kids and adults. Give them opportunities to be with others without electronic devices.

3. *Giving back*—kids learn a lot by seeing and helping others in need. It feeds the soul and teaches them about life.

4. *Sleeping and eating properly*—eating right will fuel their brains and resilience. Sleeping enough hours for their age group will give them clear minds to think and move.

5. *Talking about their feelings*—processing challenges in life out loud or on paper is imperative to building resilience. It helps them understand what they have been through and how they coped, both good and bad.

6. *Positivity*—there is power in being positive. Those who are positive by nature often live longer. Teach your children there is always something positive in any situation. This lesson will keep their brain and body healthy and a smile on their face.

7. *Imagining new possibilities*—teach your child to imagine and define their goals and support them in achieving their goals. Every child needs to imagine new possibilities and keep hope.

The American Psychological Association also adds how to bounce back when things go wrong:

1. Avoid seeing crises as insurmountable problems.
2. Accept that change is part of living.

3. Look for opportunities for self-discovery, especially when faced with hardship.

4. Keep perspective. With a significant challenge, don't lose the big picture.

Firsttee.org has a routine question that the coaches of the program ask of the kids, "Who has made a fabulous mistake we can all learn from?" That is an amazing question to learn to grow through failure. They also have the acronym FAIL as First Attempt In Learning. Teach that to your kids.

If the kids are grown, then we may have grandchildren, nieces, or nephews to teach this to. If none of the above, then remember the village.

Skills to try:

1. Look back over the first seven points and the additional four points, as well as the question and acronym. What can you teach a child?

2. You can get creative and do a home social skills class and add fun ways to teach resilience. For instance, playing musical chairs teaches you don't always win. Make a team so the kids learn to work with others. Teach kids that if they are consistently picked last, they need to find what they are good at, as God hands out gifts as He sees fit. The internet will have loads of ideas to make learning resilience fun.

Psalm 145:4a (NIV), "One generation will commend your works to another; they will tell of your mighty acts."

This is a reminder that one generation needs to tell the next generation about the wonders of God. Let's brag big time about what a mighty God we serve.

Response:

_____

_____

_____

_____

_____

_____

_____

_____

_____

_____

_____

_____

_____

_____

_____

_____

_____

Purpose

Bees Are the Bomb

Saying something is the bomb means it is very good. National Geographic and reporter Richie Hertzberg state that a honeybee's brain is only about the size of a sesame seed. Every honeybee has a job to do. Bees have to work together in different capacities to maintain a healthy nest. Some are nurses who take care of the brood; some are janitors who clean the hive, and some are forgers who gather nectar to make honey. Male bees don't work, but they spend their lives eating and waiting to mate. No comment here. Female bees are the worker bees, and they do all the work. I did not make this up. So bees are the bomb.

What is all this bee business about? It's about purpose. Bees know their purpose fully. In fact, when the female bee emerges from her larval stage, she immediately starts cleaning her cell. She is not deterred from it. God made nature very amazing. Of course, dogs, horses, and many other animals and insects know their purpose. *Oxford Dictionary* states that "purpose" is "the reason something is done, created or for which something exists." I will simply say we are designed for a reason. God does not miss a beat with us, and there are no accidents. We as adults seem to take years to find our purpose, and some never do.

Knowing and doing one's purpose creates a greater satisfaction in life. Depression, anxiety, stress, and frustration are less for those who find meaning in their life. Research indicates those fulfilling their purpose are less likely to have heart issues and dementia. If a person does not have purpose, they most likely have feelings of emptiness and hopelessness. Finding meaning helps a person get through the rough times that life dishes out and makes one feel like they can thrive and, I dare say, actually be really happy. People need to feel fulfilled and to feel like they are growing personally and contributing to something. Purpose is the cherry and whipped cream to life.

Skills to try:

1. What interests you enough to get you out of bed in the morning?

2. What are you good at? What brings you joy? What do you feel passionate about?

3. What are your core values? Your core values will guide you forward and help you make choices.

4. Ask others what they think you are good at. I asked some trusted friends and family, and they told me "counseling." I gave it considerable thought and prayer and enrolled in college for my master's degree.

5. Spend time with people who are positive, have creative ideas, have good sense, and inspire you to grow and to be a better version of yourself.

6. Are there any causes you have a heart for, such as animal welfare, social justice, seniors, children, literacy, the homeless, veterans, hospital volunteering, cancer patients, or the environment? These are only a few of the countless ones. There is also church, scouts, food banks, coaching, and companionship.

7. Start conversations with new people. Network and learn new things.

8. Pay forward. Donate your time, money, and talent to something rewarding, and while doing so, you may discover your passion. You will feel good about helping others by your volunteering. You can make a difference.

9. If you want to help bees, mix one tablespoon of water with one tablespoon of sugar and place in a shallow plate. This may be needed, as bees fly for many miles and miscalculate their journey back home, so they could be exhausted and need sustenance. I bet you will feel good helping nature.

Psalm 57:2 (NIV), "I cry out to God Most High, to God, who fulfills His purpose for me."

"God Most High" stands out as David's declaration of how sovereign God is. There is none more superior than God. He will finish what He began for all things concerning us. We have a part to play in discovering what we are called to do.

Response:

_____

_____

_____

_____

_____

_____

_____

_____

_____

_____

_____

_____

_____

_____

_____

_____

_____

_____

The Determined Lady

She started her day clothed in a lovely red and black polka dot garment. Occasionally she will change the attire to yellow or orange, but she loves wearing her polka dots. Sizewise, she is spherical and little with short legs, but she would never allow her size to deter her from what she had to do with her day. She has even well-planned what she would do if she had enemies bother her. Who or what do you think she is? She is a ladybug. Or rather, more correctly called a lady beetle. I will name her Lacy Ladybug. Her name means unbridled and cheerful. That is so true of her character. Her mission is to eat about 5,000 aphids over the course of her lifetime. She might even go the extra mile and eat some fruit flies, thrips, and mites to be helpful. If she encounters any enemies that get in the way of her fulfilling her purpose, she is prepared to secrete an oily foul-tasting fluid from her joints to keep her predators away, or she is clever enough to even play dead.

People generally want to leave a mark on society, a legacy, make a difference, make an impact in their sphere of influence, and do something they are proud of. There is a desire in all of us for our life to matter. My hope is you get there. You have it within you to find your calling. Seek, and you will find.

Albert Einstein said, "Strive not to be a success but rather to be of value."

Billy Graham stated, "God put us here for a reason—so we could come to know Him in a personal way, and then live the way He wants us to live." Not only does God have a general purpose for us, but He has a specific plan for each of our lives.

Look at possibilities that could be blocking your discovery.

1. Could it be you just don't know where to begin? In the search you know it may take time, energy, and maybe money to discover it. Does it feel like it is not worth the effort, and you will just keep things as they are so there is no struggle? Maybe you can start by volunteering where your interest lies.

2. Is there a fear holding you back? Finding your purpose might mean stepping out of your comfort zone, which can cause some fear and anxiety. It may require you to think and act outside of the box. Staying in your comfort zone helps you to potentially stay stuck and not get hurt. There is no moving forward in that case. Sticking with what is familiar may not be your friend. Henry Ford felt like his purpose was to build cars. He failed a few times, but eventually he founded the Ford Motor Company.

3. Are you struggling with doubt and insecurity? Is there uncertainty? Do you lack confidence in yourself and your abilities? Do you feel like people will judge you? Do you feel like you will disappoint others?

4. Are you sabotaging yourself? This is a self-esteem issue. You might feel like you are not worthy of achieving success, and you feel incompetent. You might even be saying that you have a negative self-image, so it confirms your negative beliefs.

5. Do you have poor coping skills? Were you told growing up that you would not amount to anything? Are you worried you will look foolish? Are you procrastinating so as to show others you can't do it? Are you prone to trying to be perfect?

6. Are you too focused on what other people will think of you? Are you going solo like you must do it alone? Seek guidance from those who have your best interest at heart and believe in you. They will also give you genuine compliments and feedback to move forward.

Your journey to discover your purpose could be so much more with the input of trusted, helpful, and wise people. These people will hopefully pray for you as well.

Skill to try:

1. Consider all of the above questions and the suggestions that pertain to you. My analogy is this: you think you want to fly with your purpose, but you have to do some planning, some predeparture things like instrument checking (that's you and some introspection). To get your plane off the ground, you have to taxi down the runway. (You have some ideas, some things you feel passionate about to take off with.) Don't allow your initial climb to burn you out by going at maximum speed. Retract the wheels (time to make adjustments for your new endeavors). Next, climb and cruise (yes, you can do it; believe in yourself) and land when necessary. Taxi to your place of refuge (really, it should be God—He has the best ideas and resources and is the One who sustains you and has created your calling). Taxi to home as well, where you give yourself some self-care and have time with family. Always take care of yourself so you go the distance.

Psalm 20:4 (NIV), "May He give you the desire of your heart and make all your plans succeed."

This psalm is attributed to David. We win in life because God desires even more than we do for us to succeed.

Response:

_____

_____

_____

_____

_____

_____

_____

_____

_____

_____

_____

_____

_____

_____

_____

_____

_____

_____

_____

_____

The Challenges and Purpose Revealed

The Bible character Joseph in Genesis 37–50 had many challenges. So do you and I, but we are not at the last chapter of our life. God has a say. Joseph had some serious family dysfunction—family that was not nurturing and full of treachery, resentment, jealousy, and hate to the point of desiring murder. Probably your family is not that bad, but you can relate to having some extreme trials. Joseph's brothers were so cold that they threw him in a cistern and then went to eat their meal. I would not be okay in a pit, as I would be thinking of any rats or snakes that shared that quarters with me. On the other hand, I know for sure that God would be aware of me and have a rescue operation in place.

Joseph's destiny was to be a leader, but he was not ready for it yet. For twenty years God worked on him and with him to get him ready for his purpose. Joseph got out of the cistern by being sold and ended up in Egypt. God had supplied his transport to where he needed to be for his purpose. No detail is missed by God. Whether in prison, a pit, or with mental or physical challenges, divine providence is at work directing your steps. God is sovereign over the universe, the physical world, the nation, human destiny, one's successes and failures, and our protection. God is responsible for us. That is great news. Joseph had many challenges, such as being imprisoned, unfairly framed, and forgotten, but like us with our many trials, we must keep the focus that God's sovereign purpose always comes into play. The lessons of becoming an overcomer were being formed in Joseph. Pharaoh noticed the Spirit of God was with him. And he prospered in all he did, so he was put in charge of everything except the throne. What happened to Joseph was wicked, but it all was working toward a greater good. Joseph was being divinely maneuvered to be in a position of authority so when there was a famine, he would save millions of people from starvation. What a purpose!

The greatest lessons of life are often the product of our most serious heartaches. Pain does not have to be meaningless. Sometimes a broken heart is the best way for God to get in and help us, and we end up comforting others. Joseph could have been full of complaints and accusations that God was not taking care of him, but he kept his faith that God was in control. Joseph was in the dungeon for years. His dungeon was a strong, dark prison. Our dungeon can mean a dark life that feels like a prison. The answer is the same for us—to trust the Lord while things look and feel dismal.

Billy Graham's wife, Ruth Bell Graham, has a remarkable saying on her tombstone, "End of construction, thank you for your patience." It is most interesting, as she must have viewed her eighty-seven years on earth as a construction project in which God was the contractor shaping her into His image and forming her for His purpose.

My most challenging situation lasted twelve years. God may have wanted to inform me how it would turn out, but that would have interrupted my spiritual growth of trust and dependency on Him. It has resulted in my being sensitive to people who are depressed and going through hard times. I love helping the underdog. God's dealings with us are sometimes mysterious. You want to get off the Rigorous Rollercoaster Ride on Roughlife Road, but look for His perspective because He will bring you through, and most likely you will find your purpose.

Dr. Andrew Newberg and Mark Waldman, neuroscientists, wrote a book called *Born to Believe*. They reported that the brain is very happy when you're focused on what you love. The more you focus on what you truly love and desire, the more the volume gets turned down in those parts of the limbic system where the destructive emotions of fear, anger, depression, and anxiety are controlled. This allows you to think more clearly. So a big clue is to focus on what we love.

Skills to try:

1. Whether a dysfunctional family is what you came from, let a new beginning, a new heritage, start with you. Let it be one that, in spite of great adversity or mental or physical challenges, it is one that holds onto faith like a dog on a bone. That means committed, tenacious, determined, ambitious, persistent, dedicated, and stubborn. You get the picture.

2. Stay the course. Keep seeking what your destiny is. Pray to get God's perspective. Be inspired.

3. To get through tests or serious life challenges, you need to remember how you respond during them will determine your outcome. Those who go through life as Carman Complainer or Donavan Doubter seem to have a hard time giving God their todays and tomorrows. They want to have their plans without God in them. How will that work? Just resigning yourself to where life is upside down is not trust. Choose trust and bypass the naysayers. Trusting God comes easier when you spend time with the Lord so He can speak help, hope, and direction to you.

I will leave this section with this little story. A family's house caught on fire, and they were getting out when their small son got scared and ran back upstairs. The father, now outside, saw his son at the upstairs window. He told him, "Jump, Son. I will catch you." But the child cried, "But, Daddy, I can't see you." The dad said, "I know, but I can see you." Isn't that wonderful? God sees us and is there with His power and help through the "smoke and fire" of our life.

Romans 12:12 (NIV), "Be joyful in hope, patient in affliction, and faithful in prayer."

You may have circumstances that do not warrant being joyful, but we can respond with joy because we have hope in the Lord. Be a person of prayer; be devoted to prayer. It's your lifeline.

Response to skills:

_____

_____

_____

_____

_____

_____

_____

_____

_____

_____

_____

_____

_____

More Help in Finding Your Purpose

"The purpose of life is to contribute in some way to making things better" (Robert F. Kennedy).

"Learn to get in touch with the silence within yourself and know that everything in life has purpose. There are no mistakes, no coincidences, all events are blessings given to us to learn from" (Elisabeth Kübler-Ross).

So many left this world and never discovered what they were in the world for. I don't want that for you. How do you know if you are the one who does something extraordinary? Or maybe it is extremely important, like raising your children to be solid citizens and contribute to society and fulfill their own purpose. Finding your purpose puts an end to boredom, as you will enjoy life and have fun. If you keep yourself focused on your goals, you will be less likely to indulge in negative habits. When moving along happily with your purpose, a person seems to have less regrets. They do not feel stagnant either.

When I was a child, people would ask me what I wanted to be when I grew up. Nobody ever got any answer out of me except "to be a mommy." Out of necessity I tried careers like hairdressing, sales, restaurant work, teaching, and counseling but that one goal loomed in my heart. To try and keep that, I delayed pursuing a career and did not get my master's degree until I was over forty years old. There was nothing wrong with that. The point is to take what time you need to search out what makes you happy and you love it so much that you can even get someone to pay you to do that career. In other words, do what you love and love what you do. Be patient with yourself, even if it takes many years to get there, but be determined to seek what fits you.

A sad tale of a man in the Bible was Samson (Judges 13–16). He had a major destiny to save Israel from Philistine oppression by his God-given strength. Samson had a problem with lust and anger. He fell in love with a woman named Delilah. She tried to trick him four times into telling her the source of his strength, but he made something up each time. Was his lust so much that he fell for this trickery each time instead of ending the nonsense? Was he daff, or did lust deter his common sense? Finally, he tells her to his peril. He was seized, and his destiny was aborted. He died. One must look at their self and see if there is sin in their life, as that could be the reason for not fulfilling one's purpose.

Look at the spiritual side—our destiny is to be like Christ. We are to show Christlikeness to our families. We are stewards of the gifts of any children God gives us. Do your children, spouse, significant others, and other family members see Christ in you? Are you the same character at home as at work and other public places? Are you Craig Crabby or Lyle Loving? Are you Ilene Irritable or Wanda Warmhearted? Here are more skills to help find your purpose. First of all, examine if sin is blocking your destiny and if you are your authentic, true self at home and everywhere you go.

Skills to try:

1. How do people describe you? If it is creative and artsy, is there an artist in you? If it is athletic, could there be a future as a pro or coach? If you play music well, is there a musician in you? If you cook well, a chef? If you like helping people with various challenges, then a social worker?

2. What can you get so absorbed in that you lose track of time? Could it be writing, building, nature, computers,

finances, sewing, designing, or the theatre?

3. What do people call on you for? Could it be mechanical, math, or gardening help? Is it fixing things, speech writing, sports help, organizing, or help with children, home decor, or training dogs?

4. What puts a smile on your face? What are you thinking of doing when you are humming or whistling? Could it be you have a lot of enthusiasm for teaching young minds?

5. As the time passes, what would you say you regretted not doing, having, or being?

6. What job do you want and why? If you want to be a model, is that realistic for you? If you love how things work or go together, can you go to school for engineering or even be an apprentice? If you love writing about traveling, is it feasible to be away?

7. If money or time were no object, what would you be doing?

8. If you could do the last five years over, what would you do differently?

9. Pretend you are bored; what would the opposite of that look like?

Colossians 3:17 (NIV), "Whatever you do, whether in word or deed, do it all in the name of the Lord Jesus, giving thanks to God, the Father through Him."

The apostle Paul gives us a great principle to live by. Are you able to say that how you are acting or what you are saying is in the name of the Lord? How do you look to the world? Are you authentic?

Response:

_____

_____

_____

_____

_____

_____

_____

_____

_____

_____

_____

_____

_____

_____

_____

_____

_____

_____

_____

_____

_____

Consider Things You Admire

"It is not enough to have lived. We should be determined to live for something" (Winston Churchill).

It's about finding out what makes you come alive. It's about discovering why you were born. One must get a vision for what one wants their life to look like, then get busy with steps to achieve that. Personally, to find mine I had to look at what touched my heart in the core of my being. First, I looked at the things I admire. For instance, I had a coworker who let her hair grow long, then she cut it and sent it off to an organization that makes wigs for cancer patients. She also volunteers with a boxing program to help people who have Parkinson's Disease. I admire the veterinarians who give free care to homeless people's pets and do free or low-cost spay and neuter and those workers who are in shelters making sure animals get in good homes. I admire first responders for the many sacrifices and medical personnel who donate their time and talent in the field. I applaud the anonymous and not anonymous gift-giving to those in need. I commend those who take care of family and friends who have chronic illnesses. I have a respect for those who share the gospel in challenging conditions and places and those who faithfully do whatever God tells them to do. This is food for thought and only a minor list for you to examine that what you admire could lead to your mission in life.

Some commendable things may be small but important. It means so much when there is a sincere prayer offered up on my behalf or on my family's behalf. Acts of kindness go a long way, such as giving a meal, dessert, or a hug. There are those who babysit, fill up a gas tank, give a ride, buy diapers and back-to-school clothes, pet sit, or pay a bill for someone. There is the faithfulness of peo-

ple to visit those in assisted living or the shut-in. There is the de-
votion of the person who teaches the disabled and those in Sunday
school, as well as the volunteer who comes and plays music. If
you admire those acts of selflessness, you may have a purpose in
serving others.

I dog walk the neighborhood twice a day and actually pass
some people's houses and ask God to bless them, or I just stop
and talk if they are outside. Those few minutes may be their only
break from loneliness. My family and I are the recipients of so
many deeds of generosity. The struggles were lessoned because
of those acts of kindness. Words of encouragement are big to a
person hurting. Things also to consider are your values, which will
help point you in a direction of a purpose. If I could only pick six
values that are admirable, they would be faith, integrity, a strong
work ethic, reverence, love, and caring. These are more ideas to
consider. What are your six values?

Along with trying to figure out what your purpose is, you must
consider timing. There could be small steps to do first, connections
to make, and finances to put in order. You may have some children
who need you a bit longer or even senior or disabled parents who
need your support before you plant your time into your mission.
Maybe you need to get to retirement or at least a work adjustment
before you jump into a new event. Your purpose may even change
over the years. In my younger years, it was all about raising my
children and doing my best to see them grow into happy, solid
citizens who love God. Today it is about ministering to those who
need help with overcoming their challenges. Hence, I am writing
a book with a mega dose of coping skills. It will always be about
God, family, friends, and others.

Skills to try:

1. Make a list of what you admire. Is there something from that list that touches you deep inside? Explore possibilities.

2. Recall when you were a recipient of an act of kindness. Can you do something for someone?

3. Thank God for the ways He has been protecting you, sustaining you, and providing for you. Express gratitude to others who have been there for you. My list is very long on both accounts. When you are being thankful, it is hard to be angry or sad at the same time.

4. Make a list of your values. This will help you figure out what is important to you, and thus, you will be more apt to make decisions aligned with them.

5. Consider how to turn your difficult past situations into a purpose. This will take you to decide that you will choose to move forward and evaluate what you learned. This includes knowing your strengths and putting your abilities to good use. For instance, did you find a bright side or positive learning curve in your divorce, bankruptcy, job loss, abuse, miscarriage, health scare, or death of a loved one? When you don't feel the pain or anger anymore, you are likely ready to help others.

Proverbs 19:17 (NIV), "He who is kind to the poor lends to the Lord, and He will reward him for what he has done."

We can never lose when we give to the Lord. Helping is so important to God that He chooses to bless the giver.

Response:

_____

_____

_____

_____

_____

_____

_____

_____

_____

_____

_____

_____

_____

_____

_____

_____

_____

_____

Burnout

Jethro and the Llama

Picture yourself in a beautiful car of your choosing, and you are ready to take it for a spin. Get a visual now. However, there is a problem; it won't start! Everything is new, and no mechanics are at fault. What could be wrong? Well, there is no gas in the tank. This is a comparison to you being the beautiful car, and you can't go because you are burned out. Do you feel like you are close to empty or already on empty? "Empty" means "containing nothing, not filled, or lacking meaning." Maybe you have seen your check engine light come on, and you ignored it. That light blinks or stays on until it is fixed, so you may have really ignored taking care of yourself.

Burnout defined is a form of exhaustion caused by constantly feeling swamped. It's a result of excessive and prolonged emotional, physical, or mental stress. It happens when you're overwhelmed, emotionally drained, and unable to keep up with life's incessant demands. Burnout keeps you from being productive. It reduces your energy, making you feel hopeless, cynical, and resentful. The effects of burnout can hurt your home, work, and social life. Long-term burnout can make you more vulnerable to colds and flu.

WebMD, December 3, 2020

Let's deal with work burnout. There are seven work burnout types, according to an article in the US News, February 2021. One is being an overachiever. This is when you chase trying to get a promotion, for example, rather than enjoy the process. Burnout type two is a taskmaster in which you drive yourself to keep working, a focus on doing instead of being. Burnout type three is being a perfectionist—your thought is anything less than perfect is a failure. Type four is a micromanager/controller. This person has a lack of trust in anyone but themselves and has trouble dealing with the unknown. Burnout type five is the competitor. This individual does whatever it takes to win or succeed at all costs. Burnout type six is the people pleaser. The root cause is the belief that saying yes will avoid disappointing or hurting others. And the last burnout type is the ruminator. This one mistakenly believes that focusing intently on a problem will solve it or at least relieve the discomfort of not knowing the answer.

On the other hand, caregiver burnout has its challenges to one's mental and physical health as well. This individual is experiencing physical, mental, or emotional exhaustion. This stressed caregiver may have anxiety and depression. It can be so debilitating that the caregiver may become negative instead of caring even if they don't mean to be. The caregiver usually doesn't get the help they need, or they do more than they are able, physically or financially. They also may have trouble separating their roles as spouses, lovers, children, friends, and other close relationships. Caregivers expect that what they do has a positive role on the patient, but it could be unrealistic if it is a patient with a progressive disease. Many caregivers get frustrated by a lack of money, resources, and skills to effectively plan, manage, and organize the loved one's care. Some caregivers place unreasonable demands upon themselves because they see providing care as their exclusive responsibility (Cleveland Clinic).

Do you recognize yourself as having work burnout or caregiver burnout or even both? So let's say we have an emotional and physical gas tank. We are not going anywhere with it empty. Not only can we experience anxiety and depression as mentioned, but now add hopelessness.

Now about the llama that is in the title. Llamas know their limits. If you try and overload them too much, they may just lie down and refuse to move. Just because they are strong doesn't mean they should carry more load. When they are agitated or their patience is being tested, the llama may decline to work. They are a good companion and willing to do the heavy lifting. Take notice of their spit, which can be flung ten feet or more. They will respond to fairness and good care. It seems like we are similar.

Jethro, also in the title, is the father-in-law to Moses. He seemed to know a lot about Moses' character, as Moses worked for him for forty years. Jethro came to Moses and observed Moses sitting to judge the people from morning until evening. Moses defended this practice as the people needed help to seek God's will, and he was there to settle disputes. Jethro gave solid advice and told Moses this would wear him out. He suggested he select capable men to serve over the people and only Moses handle the most difficult cases (Exodus 18:17). Jethro is an example of someone who knew how to delegate. Many people find this difficult to do.

Skills to try:

1. Check the burnout descriptions above and see if any of them describes you. If so, what modifications can you make to your time or to being with people who could be draining you?

2. If the load is too much, as illustrated by the llama example, can you just sit down and make adjustments where necessary? Do this before any spitting that might occur!

3. Surround yourself with wise and caring people like Jethro. Listen and consider their advice, as it is coming from a place of love and concern for your well-being.

4. You are drained of emotional and physical gas when depleted. Keep your gas tank from becoming empty by self-care. Do things like find some solitude so you can rest, repair, and recharge. Carve out time for your hobby and do something that makes you feel good.

5. Watch out for your negative thinking, which can come easy when so weary and under great pressure. Speak back to it. Speak the Word of God.

6. Meditate/pray. The Lord is completely able to refresh you and strengthen you. This means you cannot be a one-man or one-woman everything. Jethro told Moses that was not good. You have an invitation always to come to the Lord, who can revive your drained soul and your out-of-gas body.

Jeremiah 31:25 (NIV), "I will refresh the weary and satisfy the faint."

The Lord does this so well that we will lack nothing. He can also restore our joy and hope.

Response:

_____

_____

_____

_____

_____

_____

_____

_____

_____

_____

_____

_____

_____

_____

_____

_____

_____

_____

Delegate and Say No

This is not the kind of "no" like Ebenezer Scrooge would say but the kind that gives you some respect and will help decrease burnout.

As you have probably watched *A Christmas Carol* by Charles Dickens some time in your life, you know that Ebenezer Scrooge was a cold-hearted, selfish, greedy, lonely miser who was disgusted with Christmas. He was incredibly unkind to his underpaid clerk, Bob Cratchit, who needed money for his very ill son. He would not even put enough coal in the clerk's office to keep him warm. When Mr. Cratchit asked for Christmas off, Scrooge resented it but allowed it only if he came in early the next morning to make up some time. Scrooge even said "no" to a charity worker who asked for a donation for the poor. He went too far by voicing his opinion that "Perhaps prison might be a better venue for the poor." Oh my, oh my! Fortunately, he later turned around from loathsome to a changed man who shared his generosity with everyone.

For the business world, delegating is a must. A person can't and shouldn't do everything themself. Delegating to others in the business sector means you empower others and build trust in them. A good example is Colin Powell, who had the highest position in the Department of Defense. He had to delegate to his chiefs of staff in Iraq. It was a time of war, and General Powell stated that he chose to trust his staff to do the right thing. There was a lot at stake.

Former President Ronald Reagan has been dubbed the "Great Delegator." His secret to success was that he delegated to those he put in authority, and when he needed something, he asked specifically. He made goals that were very clear, then assigned them to

312

"his fellas."

The reasons why some business people may not choose to delegate are: they lack faith in others, they have trouble with anyone who may not give 100 percent, they do not plan ahead, they fear failure, they view reduction in their workload as a threat to their ego or self-worth, or they are overly attached to their habit or routine (Matthew Dicks, August 6, 2015). Other reasons for not delegating are the person in charge may feel they would lose control, they desire the limelight, they do not know how to delegate, or they don't want to take the time to oversee the person.

Caregivers have a high-stress job. Unlike the business person who can leave work at the end of the day, the caregiver may be on duty all day and night. The caregiver needs a life outside of caregiving. Not only is there the twenty-four seven of the job, but they may be watching their loved one decline, and they are aware of what may be the final outcome. This can bring on a significant amount of stress and depression. Calling in resources in family and friends and using respite care are vital.

When I worked for the sheriff's department and dealt with inmates, it was a regular thing for them to ask me for things they wanted. I would go out of my way to accommodate them the best I was allowed, such as getting them a book or an inmate pen. However, they knew from their handbook what they could not have and yet still would ask. My answer to them was, "It's not happening." I felt like my frankness still came across as "Sorry. I care, but I cannot do that." Respect was maintained. They also knew my "it's not happening" was not wishy-washy and that it would not turn into a maybe. You do the right thing because it is the right thing to do.

For the caregiver and the business manager, saying "no" is oftentimes hard to do. Damon Zahariades from *The Art of Saying No* offers these worthy insights:

People have been conditioned to say "yes." As kids we said no to parents and teachers and received negative feedback, so we said "yes" more often. We made friends by saying "yes," and we said "yes" in our career path with every opportunity in the hopes of getting ahead.

Damon suggests these ways to say "no":

1. If you say "yes" to anyone and everything, you'll have "no" time to focus on your needs. You will be overwhelmed, stressed, exhausted, and feel bitter and resentful towards the people taking up your time.

2. We value things that are hard to attain, so if your friends and coworkers know you do not freely give away your time, they will appreciate your time more.

3. Every time you say "yes" you could be saying "no" to something you value. The next time you are about to say "yes" to a time-consuming request to please someone, remember the three P's: people, project and personal well-being. This is how it works:

   • Imagine saying "no" to the people you want to spend time with and see the disappointment on their faces.

   • Imagine not having the satisfaction of completing that one project you're passionate about.

   • Imagine seeing yourself a week from now, burnt out and exhausted because you said "no" to the activities that would help you recharge, recover, and improve your personal wellbeing.

Added insight from Damon on how to say "no" without angering people:

1. Categorial nos—"When you give someone a categorical 'no' by saying, 'I've stopped,' or 'I don't,' you make

your 'no' seem like an objective fact and not a personal rejection."

2. Commitments—"When you say 'no' by referencing a commitment, people are generally understanding and rarely push back."

3. Counteroffers—"Instead of saying 'no' to someone's request, especially someone whose relationship you value greatly, say 'no' to their initial request and counter with a smaller offer."

Skill to try:

1. Look at the suggestions for saying "no" and see if you can practice some if applicable. Life needs to be in balance. The goal is to take care of necessary situations but not get burned out.

Psalm 68:19 (NIV), "Praise be to the Lord, to God our savior; who daily bears our burdens."

We go through life and have responsibilities, such as caring for loved ones and even ourselves. His promise is He will lift our burdens. Release the weight on your shoulders to the Lord.

Response:

Gratitude

Don't Forget Your Saucer

Do you think every cup needs a saucer? It will be a "yes" if you believe the contents of what's in your cup will overflow onto the saucer. It means you have more than enough. That sounds like a wonderful analogy of God's generosity. It's about His excess of love, blessings, and power. Our response to that should be gratitude, which is the quality of being thankful. It's about living in the overflow. It is being included for this lesson because it is a positive emotion that is beneficial to us mentally and physically. Grateful people are happier people.

Consider listening to a song from Michael Combs called "Drinking from My Saucer," as it has a good message.

Gratitude can boost serotonin and dopamine (the brain's pleasure center). It's a great formula—think grateful, positive thoughts, and feel more content. When you are filled with positive thoughts, every area of your life will be affected. You can get through the challenges of life better as Poppy Positive instead of Uri Ungrateful.

Courtney Ackerman, in PositivePsychology.com, April 12,

2017, wrote about the benefits of gratitude. Some of those included are:

1. "We will be happier. Journaling helps one to notice what they already have that can make one be more positive."

2. "Researcher Chic-Che Lin records that a high level of gratitude has a strong impact on one's psychological well-being, self-esteem and depression."

3. "Gratitude reduces envy, facilitates positive emotions, and makes·us more resilient."

4. "Gratitude is a protective factor when it comes to suicide ideation in stressed and depressed individuals."

5. "There are social benefits such as a wider social network, more friends, and better relationships."

6. "Expressing gratitude to our friends can improve [relationships]. They are more likely to work through problems and concerns."

7. "Gratitude can make us more optimistic. The more we think about what we are grateful for, the more we find to be grateful for."

8. "Practicing gratitude can help you get out of any spiritual funk. The more spiritual you are, the more likely you are to be grateful, and vice versa."

9. "It can decrease one's self-centeredness. One is more likely to share with others, even at the expense of themselves, and even if the receiver was a stranger."

10. "Those who are the most grateful tend to be less materialistic and they enjoy greater life satisfaction."

11. "In the work place gratitude enhances managerial skills, enhances your praise-giving and motivating abilities as a mentor."

12. "It helps a person find meaning in their job, along with applying their strengths, positive emotions and flow, hope, and finding a 'calling.'"

13. "Gratitude and respect in the workplace can help em-

ployees feel embedded in their organization, or welcomed and valued."

14. "People with hypertension who 'count their blessings' at least once a week experience a significant decrease in blood pressure, resulting in better overall health. I recommend daily counting your blessings."

15. "It can play a role in recovery from substance use or abuse."

"It's a funny thing about life, once you begin to take note of the things you are grateful for, you begin to lose sight of the things you lack" (Germany Kent).

Skills to try:

1. Gratitude is a choice. Start with deliberately choosing to start your day with gratitude, appreciation, and thanks.

2. Think about the people, places, and things that you are grateful for. Add your health and the health of your loved ones. Express to others out loud, in a letter, or in a prayer something you are grateful for. You can say you are grateful for their support, encouragement, prayers, time, guidance, gifts, wisdom, or how they have made a difference in your life.

3. Thank God for the multitude of things you are grateful for. Listen to the song "10,000 Reasons to Bless the Lord" by Matt Redman for inspiration.

4. Look around at the beauty of nature. Can you take it all in and see His magnificence in the mountains, breeze, trees, rainbows, northern lights, rain, clouds, ocean, and waterfalls? Do an experiment and document how much you can notice. Don't forget to include the critters.

Psalm 23:5b-6 (NIV), "My cup overflows, surely goodness and love will follow me all the days of my life, and I will dwell in the house of the Lord forever."

A cup running over is symbolic of joy. For you to dwell in the house of the Lord forever, you have to be sure He is your Shepherd.

Response:

_____

_____

_____

_____

_____

_____

_____

_____

_____

_____

_____

_____

_____

_____

_____

Be Sure You Return

Have you ever thought about what it would be like to have an incurable disease and be ostracized from people? You have to leave your family and go and live with other contagious and probably terminal people. You cannot go buy food, shop for clothes, or go to a church or meeting; thus, you become a beggar. Your skin is thick and crusty with sores. Disfigurement begins as you lose some fingers and toes. You have a lot of pain from the nerve damage. You are considered to be low on society's totem pole. It is somewhat of a graphic description, but there is a point to be made here, so please follow me. This is a description of a person who had leprosy in ancient times. Imagine the very sadness and suffering of this life as an outcast.

There is a great story in Luke 17:12–19 about Jesus encountering ten men who had leprosy. These ten actually asked for pity; they wanted to be healed. Jesus told them to go and show themselves to the priest, and on the way all ten were healed. This might have been a test of faith. Only one returned to say thank you. In fact, his gratitude was so great that he came and praised God in a loud voice and threw himself at Jesus' feet. I like to write so people get a visual. If I was the one who had to live the rest of my life as an outcast and my body was hideous and disfigured to the point my limbs were lost, I would be beyond grateful.

This is about gratitude. Life is a gift. Those who have been healed or restored much love much and are especially grateful for much. There is a difference between thanks and gratitude. The difference is how they are used. Giving thanks involves being aware of the actions of another, such as "thank you for the lovely meal" or "thank you for giving me a ride." You acknowledge something.

Gratitude goes much deeper and seems to imply you are impacted by another person or thing. There is something that has made a difference in your life. For instance, over the course of the years, I have had a lot of financial challenges that were not of my doing. I have been given money to pay my bills, to which I expressed my gratitude. That was big and life-changing. Otherwise, who knows what negative situations would have come of that? One of those magnanimous gifts came from my three very generous sons.

The greatest expression of gratitude should be to the Lord for dying an excruciating death on the cross so we are saved from eternity in hell and can be restored to a right relationship with God. We can be like the one who had leprosy and gave praise and fell at His feet with gratitude. We can live a life worthy of the work of the cross and serve and honor Him all the days of our life.

> *Acts of generosity and kindness make a difference to the receiver, the giver, and to anyone who witnessed the exchange or hears the story later. Everyone connected to generosity wins. There are seven forms of generosity: thoughts, words, money, time, things, influence, and attention.*

Trinity Family Wealth

Having generous thoughts can involve not being negative to others or oneself. Being generous can divert away from our critical inner voice as well as help us not judge others. To give attention is to fully tune in to others and be good listeners. We need to choose words that show we care. Encouragement and sincere compliments are free. Influencing others in an appropriate way may include things such as how to develop a work ethic, have a giving spirit, have faith, or be a good parent. There can be an influence of how to treat people right, such as not bullying or respect for differences. How about the influence of love and compassion by giving a hand up and improving someone's living situation? One might choose to influence others in how to play a sport and develop good sportsmanship. Giving of your time can be about anything. There are so many for me to mention, but family and friends have painted our house and patio, uninstalled and reinstalled a dishwasher and micro hood, righted a tree bent over by a hurricane, and bought me a plane ticket to pick up my husband in the hospital from out of state. We have been multiple times blessed by others' time and talents.

Skills to try:

1. Share your stories of generosity with your family to help them develop this attribute.

2. Model generosity. Teach your children to share their time and their belongings.

3. Be a good Samaritan. Can you buy a meal, groceries, clothes, or medicine for someone? Can you pay for someone's haircut, buy school supplies, or give a ride? Can you give money to keep a person's utilities on? Can you pay for a car or home repair? Be sure to expect nothing in return. You will know what works for you to do. A small or big gesture counts.

4. Remember that companionship is a generous gift of your time. Do you know someone lonely, fighting an illness, or shut in to spend some time with? Maybe someone is having a rough patch and just needs an expression of love.

5. Can you help others with your time and talent to achieve their goals and dreams?

6. What are the ways you can be a good influence on others?

7. Give to causes, charities, missionaries, shelters, and churches. Volunteer. People and animals need us.

Proverbs 11:25 (NIV), "A generous man will prosper; he who refreshes others will himself be refreshed."

The Lord rewards us. We are to be a source of refreshment to others. God sees it and sees to it that we are restored, strengthened, fortified, and blessed. He can breathe life into us and our circumstances.

Response:

Moving Toward Being Happier

Design Your Floor Plan

"Home is made of bricks and beams. A home is made of hopes and dreams" (Ralph Waldo Emerson).

The thing about life is to change what you are not satisfied with. Don't try and be, do, and have what is not going to make you happy. Be you, accept yourself, and love yourself.

Consider designing your life like you would design a floor plan. You are going to design this home (your life) with some features (needs and wants) you must have. Get some vision, make goals, and have enthusiasm. What ideas do you have? Are they realistic plans (realistic goals for your life)? Do you need four bedrooms when two or three will do? Do you want skylights because you need the sunlight coming in? What features will make you happy?

I will build my floor plan so you get the idea, then you try building yours. The floor plan must include the security of solid doors and impact windows. My associations are with people that I feel safe around. They love, respect, appreciate, trust and accept

325

me, and vice versa. We feel blessed to have each other. I would need my own space, like a spare room or craft room, where I can pray, read, type, unwind, and have time for solitude. Having hobbies is healthy. A playroom for the grandchildren would be fun. The master bedroom is a place of reprieve and rest. Intimacy has importance. We all want to feel loved and experience love played out in positive communication, both physically and emotionally. Self-esteem will be built or lost there but hopefully built. Of course, plan your room even if there is no significant other. Two bathrooms are necessary. The kitchen is the place of communication: talking about your day, making plans, and helping one another. The family room would be the hub where my guests and I enjoy sharing, laughing, playing, snacking, and relaxing. My dog would be somewhere nearby. A must is a porch where nature beckons. I need to see flowers, trees, and butterflies and feel the sun or breeze. My stressors dissipate when there.

So I listed safety, strong friendships and family connections, and feeling loved, respected, accepted, appreciated, trusted, and affirmed. There is time for me to relax, play, talk, laugh, and communicate intimately. I am healthy when I have my pet, interests to pursue, or nature to enjoy.

You might have a pretty good idea of how you want your design (life) to go, but don't forget the outside. How do you want to look to others? Before you say you don't care what others think, remember you feel better emotionally and physically when you are freshly cleaned up, just like a house with a good-looking exterior. Sometimes when a person has depression, there is a struggle to do mundane hygiene tasks. That could be due to lack of energy, motivation that is close to nil, or a sensory processing disorder.

Just for fun, look at all the kinds of exteriors, such as vinyl, brick, stucco, stone, wood, or metal. Each has something about it that would make one choose that particular material. For instance, vinyl is popular and requires minimal maintenance. Brick is good for those who like a Colonial, Tudor, or English cottage look. Stucco is durable and has an earthy feel. Wood can be elegant and last a long time, but critters might eat away at it. When you choose a paint color, it says a lot about your personality. If you choose a yellow color, you are probably optimistic; choose white—you are neat; brown, you may be lowkey; green, you are not flashy; beige, you like no frills; or pink, you are creative. Blue is a color choice of those who like to return home to calm when the world is chaotic.

Skill to try:

1. Design your floor plan (life). You are the architect. Get a contractor or two (friends and family). What materials will you need or want? Be open to new resources.

Isaiah 32:18 (NIV), "My people will live in peaceful dwelling places, in secure homes, in undisturbed places of rest."

Oh, how wonderful to dwell in safety where we do not have fear but have peace and rest.

Response:

_____

_____

_____

_____

_____

_____

_____

_____

_____

_____

_____

_____

_____

_____

_____

_____

_____

_____

"Don't Worry, Be Happy"

This is the title to a song by Bobby McFerrin. It was a cappella, and he used his body to make the sounds. It is recorded that he just liked the philosophy of those four little words.

It is a bit pie in the sky, as life is not so simple and optimistic. The opposite of happy is unhappy, sad, miserable, depressed, unfortunate, or disturbed. Being happy may not be so easy to achieve, or is it? Ask yourself, "Am I living the life I want? Am I feeling fulfilled in my current life circumstance? Am I positive? Are my relationships going well? Do I have enough money and necessities to maintain life in a way that is full of enjoyable activities? Have I created a beautiful and comfortable home? Do I participate in things that I value? Am I bettering myself and improving the world around me? Do I feel alive? Do I regularly express gratitude?" For this list of ten questions, if you are predominately saying "no," then are you willing to make changes?

Here are a couple of notable cartoon characters: Charlie Brown, from the Peanuts comic strip, the longsuffering but lovable loser, and Eeyore the donkey, a friend of Christopher Robin's from Winnie the Pooh. Charlie Brown is uncertain, uncomfortable in his own skin, and sometimes afraid. He is scoffed at and taken advantage of and has a bunch of insecurities. His notable quotes are "Awkward is my specialty" and "My anxieties have anxieties." Eeyore is quite miserable, pessimistic, and chronically depressed, and he struggles to give and receive love. He has a notable tail that is nailed on. One of his famous quotes is, "Don't worry about me. Go and enjoy yourself. I'll stay here and be miserable."

The purpose of including these two fictional characters is to see if you relate in such a way as to act like them. That would be a reason you are unhappy. We all can probably relate to some extent. Look at the places where something you may be doing or thinking is contributing to a life less desirable. What can you do to move out of that behavior and stop the negative thinking?

Are you blocking yourself from loving and being loved? This is evidenced by not receiving a compliment, trying to redirect any focus on you to elsewhere, shying away, or making excuses for not receiving affection. Feeling unlovable or that you don't deserve love is a self-esteem concern but also a block to giving and receiving love. Fear of getting hurt will hold you back. This is part of trusting your instincts. The person who may have hurt you in the past is not the person right before you. More than likely, the new person really likes you, likes your personality and your looks, and finds you enjoyable to be with. Work on any issues you have with a history of abandonment. This is an attachment issue and causes insecurity and feelings one will be rejected. If it is deep-rooted or if there is depression or anxiety holding you back, then consult a mental health therapist. Refer to the sections in this book on dealing with depression and anxiety.

Skills to try:

1. If feeling empty, consider the Lord can fill the empty places. He is the One who will never do you wrong. We are made of body, soul, and spirit, and the spirit often gets neglected.

2. Don't try to get people to accept and love you. Let it flow naturally. Do not dwell on your flaws. Build your self-worth, and you will see that you will attract what you think you deserve.

3. You are with yourself twenty-four hours a day, so love yourself and take care of yourself. We all struggle. We must show ourselves compassion. Do not berate yourself. We are all human.

4. Give yourself some treats/gifts. I am a chocolate kind of girl, and I know to do this.

5. Give yourself a break and forgive yourself. It is hard to move forward if you don't do this.

6. Accept your imperfections. Got a "nailed-on tail" like Eeyore—don't hone in on it but accept yourself. People will look at you as real. Don't hide away. Eeyore put a bow on his tail. That was very cool of him.

7. Some people will not like you. Accept that. Lucy is supposedly a friend of Charlie's, but she is mean and calls him names. Set boundaries with people who treat you badly. No compromising.

8. To receive love, you will need to be vulnerable. This is a "take it kind of slow" thing. Know what to share and when. Allow a healing in any areas where there have been wounds.

9. Don't let any fear of rejection hold you back and get control over you. Don't be defensive.

10. Can you help another with their self-esteem while you work on yours? Give sincere compliments and positive feedback and remind them of their strengths and assets. Involve them so they can see they have something to contribute. You will feel happier when you help others.

11. To combat insecurity, you should be present with your current relationship. Don't dwell on past relationship mistakes. It's a waste of time and energy and takes away from what is before you.

12. Watch out for your inner critic. Sometimes we are not nice to ourselves or have a self-fulling prophecy that nobody could like us or that a new friend is going to leave. Change the focus and tell yourself something positive about yourself. Pretend you have a box in the closet or even a bingo cage, and put the negative critic in its place. At least this may quiet it.

13. Get some paper and on the left side write the changes you know you need to make to create more happiness.

On the right side, across from each, write the plan of action to accomplish that.

Psalm 73:26 (NIV), "My flesh and my heart may fail, but God is the strength of my heart and my portion forever."

Physically and mentally, we may fail, but God is our refuge, our strength that never fails. Saying He is my portion forever means He is our inheritance, our source of security and hope.

Response:

_____

_____

_____

_____

_____

_____

_____

_____

_____

_____

_____

_____

_____

_____

Anticipation Is Like a Chocolate Lab

Anticipation is such a great coping strategy that it is like having a great temperament dog, such as a chocolate Labrador. Before you think it is an odd comparison, look at it this way—anticipation is an emotion that causes excitement about something that is going to happen, and chocolate labs are good companions, happy, friendly, affectionate, agile, and sweet. Anticipation causes positive feelings, so we naturally have less negative feelings. It also gives us something to look forward to, so we have a sense of well-being. A chocolate lab is ready for excitement and adventure anytime; they are active, curious, and full of spirit and energy. You may be having a low-mood day and can tell yourself, "No, I will choose to have a chocolate lab day."

Positive feelings decrease painful feelings. When we expect good outcomes, there is a release of dopamine in the brain. Positive feelings can create a feeling of euphoria. That will help you get through stressful events. Anticipation also helps to release the active reward center of the brain. Greg Kushnick, a New York psychiatrist, reports that anticipation generates hopeful feelings; it makes uncertainty more manageable, gives us hope and a sense of control, and helps us know that positive emotions will happen in the future.

The reward center in our brain is a big deal. It drives our behavior toward pleasurable stimuli, such as food, sex, alcohol, shopping, and social media. It drives us away from painful ones that require more energy or effort, such as conflict. At the center of the reward system is a region of the brain called the striatum, which coordinates the value of the stimulus in a nanosecond, sending "go for it" or "stay away from it" signals. Dopamine is the "go get it" neurochemical that drives us to stimuli or rewards and behaviors that we need for survival. The feeling of pleasure comes from natural opioids in the brain that produce a feeling of euphoria or a high. Dopamine and opioids work together (The Reward Foundation).

With anticipation we are going to be jovial, but there is another side, which is anticipatory anxiety. It is the dread one experiences before an event. The body seems to respond to a perceived threat, and that individual could be close to being panic-stricken. An example would be you are looking forward to a date but are anxious about the unknown, or you are happy about going on vacation but have some dread about the traffic. That one is me. In comparison to the chocolate lab, these dogs are so fun, easygoing, and enjoy family time (positive anticipation), but they can get "hotspots," which are a painful, very itchy skin condition that gets worse as the dog scratches it (like anticipatory anxiety).

There are four feel-good hormones—serotonin, endorphins, oxytocin, and dopamine, which is called the happy hormone and the main one that drives the brain's reward center. To keep my happy feelings going, I look for the things that make me cheerful. The small things are: my grandchildren coming for a visit, the day of my favorite television show, a plan to go to a craft fair, and seeing a friend and having lunch or going shopping. I am also jovial when I hear the music at church.

The big event that keeps my reward center in a "go for it" mood is planning a vacation and going. This keeps me joyful for weeks, as there is the internet search for a cabin and places to see to play being a tourist, as well as restaurants to review. Once there, my brain's dopamine production continues, as there is the scenery, hiking, and unique shops to explore. When I give myself time to meditate/pray, the brain will release more dopamine. That is a win-win. My dog goes with us, and she is the best little animal at making me a happy person.

AnxietyCanada.com has made these suggestions to help minimize any potential for negative anticipatory anxiety:

1. Ask family and friends to give you some warning about any upcoming events.
2. Focus on the fun and positive aspect of the pending event.
3. Remind yourself that any physical sensations you have when anxious are harmless.
4. Learn to relax, tolerate uncertainty, and practice balanced thinking.

Skills to try:

1. Every day try to find a small something to look forward to so the happy feelings continue.
2. At the end of the day, write down something you are looking forward to for the next day.
3. Make exciting plans, large and small, and relish each moment.
4. Avoid negative routine as much as possible to keep you out of a rut.

Psalm 16:11 (NIV), "You have made known to me the path of life; You will fill me with joy in your presence, with eternal pleasures at your right hand."

David is celebrating his relationship with the Lord. Commune with the Lord and experience joy.

Response:

_____
_____
_____
_____
_____
_____
_____
_____
_____
_____
_____
_____
_____
_____
_____
_____
_____
_____
_____
_____
_____

Get in the Dirt

What do you get when you cross a four-leaf clover with poison ivy? The answer is a rash of bad luck.

What is small, red, and whispers? The answer is a hoarse radish.

The title refers to the dirt of the earth, not the dirt as in gossip. Something that de-stresses me big time is to be in my garden. I am one of those people who plant flowers and pull weeds with no gloves on just to feel the earth. Dirt under my nails is no problem because, of course, I will give myself a manicure. I pull the weeds and sing a praise song to the Lord and pray as well. How can you not leave that case scenario feeling less stressed? I have a butterfly garden and a few flower gardens. Almost daily I check for caterpillars. I can sit on my porch and look at the colors in my hydrangeas, daisies, crown of thorns, geraniums, petunias, etcetera. I have a small waterfall to add sound as well, and I can hear the song of birds. There is a little bush of cherry tomatoes. The sun and breeze seem like they kiss my skin. There is a lovely aroma. Gardening touches all the senses of sight, smell, touch, hearing, and taste.

Does any of that delightful commentary make you want to send out for new seeds or visit a garden department and get started? Have you considered a garden walk, being part of a garden club, or a community garden? Many schools would love to have someone start a garden. Have you considered the health benefits of gardening, like increasing serotonin and decreasing cortisol? How about building strength? A half hour in the sun produces between ten to twenty thousand international units of vitamin D in your body. Vitamin D helps regulate one's immune system. Vitamin D helps your body absorb calcium, which is essential for bone health.

Gardening gives purpose: the plants need care. Guests who come to our home know they have to check out the latest in my garden endeavors. If you are not an avid gardener, then consider a class to get you started, and it is almost guaranteed you will make a friend of someone you ask to help you get going.

Does it seem like with all that wonderfulness you may not be successful, or you wonder about the time versus reward of it? There is a learning curve. I have killed plants by accident, and it has taken several attempts to get any delightful vegetables. So I had to stick with what is easy to grow like green beans. Each time there is something new to learn, which makes me feel more proficient. With gardening you can be very creative. It is a great skill to teach your children about science and ecosystems. Flowers attract birds, bees, and wildlife for a healthy ecosystem.

> *"I like gardening—it's a place where I find myself when I need to lose myself" (Alice Sebold).*

> *"You can bury any number of headaches in a garden" (Charles Barnard, 1889).*

Skills to try:

1. Start a garden: vegetable, flower, butterfly, organic, or herb. Ask others about their skills and educate yourself.
2. Consider this poem or make one up about how you feel about your garden. It is called "Gardener's Prayer":

   Thank you, God for sun and showers,

   Thank you, God for each lovely flower,

   Thank you for each stately tree,

   Through all of these you speak to me.

Ecclesiastes 2:5 (NIV), "I made me gardens and parks, and I planted all kinds of fruit trees in them."

King Solomon wrote this. He had it all. This verse alludes to his choice to build a garden, as he found pleasure in it.

Response:

_____

_____

_____

_____

_____

_____

_____

_____

_____

_____

_____

_____

_____

_____

_____

_____

Get Your Cuddle On

Randolph Schmid, June 18, 2008, wrote a piece for *The Associated Press* about chimpanzees that were victims of aggression and what helped them. It was reported that research demonstrated that hugs and kisses helped lower stress when a third chimp stepped in and offered consolation. If a kiss was given, it was usually on the top of the head or on their back. If an embrace, the consoler chimp would wrap one or both arms around the recipient. Consolation, which is providing comfort to a person who has suffered, and cuddling reduce stress. We knew that, but now we must add that some animals benefit from this as well.

This is my attempt to inform you about the "love and trust" hormone and its role in decreasing stress, anxiety, and depression. Research is ongoing, and I am not a medical professional but a licensed mental health professional with significant knowledge on what can improve the mood. One such hormone is called oxytocin. And by the way, you do want this good thing. It's what is behind attraction and some aspects of the reproductive system.

The hypothalamus produces oxytocin and sends it to the pituitary gland. From there it is released into the bloodstream. So what does that have to do with helping you feel more alive? It has the power to regulate one's emotional responses and social behaviors. It will help create connections with others. It assists a person in developing trust, empathy, positive memories, and communication. Get oxytocin to work with your feel-good neurotransmitters serotonin and dopamine, and you have a case of the warm and fuzzies, and from there "the happy dance" and who knows what.

During labor oxytocin stimulates the muscles of the uterus to contract, and it helps after childbirth with mother-and-child bonding while breastfeeding. Low levels of oxytocin are linked with postpartum depression.

People who are struggling with stress and depression see life and love differently. All that negativity and worry causes cortisol to be secreted. Oxytocin will promote the secretion of serotonin and dopamine, which will help build resistance to stress. It protects the nervous system from shutting down so you don't want to flee. Research states oxytocin helps relieve pain as well.

Oxytocin is also called the social hormone. If you are not socializing, you might have low oxytocin. If you are introverted or have social anxiety, there could be a connection with your levels. You might also exhibit poor communication. Your libido may be slow. You might crave sugar. When oxytocin cells in the brain are blunted, your body seeks out sweets. Levels also might be low if you are distrustful (Romper.com by Yvette Manes). You might find it easy to disconnect from people. Low levels can also cause you to not feel good about yourself.

For a person who does not have a significant other, there are pets or other close friends. For those who are not used to cuddling, then go at it slow enough for your comfort level and just start with little touches. Verbal expressions of affection are quite positive. Another way to boost oxytocin is to exercise or enjoy music. For example, singing in a group is bonding.

Skills to try:

1. Hug, kiss, flirt, cuddle, give a back rub, hold hands, put your head on your partner, "spoon," and look in someone's eyes who you are attracted to. Be adventurous and amorous.
2. Hug, kiss, and give belly rubs to the dog, cat, bunny, horse, bird, or other animals you love.

3. Get a massage. A massage is relaxing as well as helps lower the levels of stress hormones and boosts the feel-good neurotransmitters.

4. Take B vitamins and magnesium. Low levels of B12 and other B vitamins, such as B6, may be linked to depression. Magnesium blocks the stimulating neurotransmitters and binds them to calming receptors, resulting in a more peaceful, resting state.

5. Get in the water, the sun, or nature. Exercise, dance, listen to music, do something fun.

6. Connect with friends or loved ones.

7. Eat foods with tryptophan (eggs, bananas, yogurt, salmon, walnuts, cashews, potatoes). Your body makes L-tryptophan into serotonin, which helps control your mood and sleep.

Hebrews 10:24–25a (NIV), "Let us consider how we may spur one another on toward love and good deeds. Let us not give up meeting together, as some are in the habit of doing."

"One another" seems to mean "reciprocal." Getting to know one another leads to love, good works, and positive interactions in general.

Response:

The Rootbound Family

The Rootbound family is a good, loving family, but they all seem rather morose. Mrs. Roxanne Rootbound is bored and ambivalent. Mr. Roy Rootbound feels stagnant and just goes through his routine rather unmotivated. The daughter, Romina, does not seem to care about much and feels unfulfilled, and the son, Rory, has lost his creative edge and is barely attending school, as if it is pointless. This is a description of being in a rut. That rut, defined by *Oxford Dictionary*, is "a habit or pattern of behavior that has become dull and unproductive, but hard to change." This family is experiencing the doldrums. They do not have anything interesting going on and nothing to look forward to. None of them have anything in particular they are working toward in the way of goals, as every day is about the same.

Let's compare this family to a plant by their name's sake, one that is root bound. This plant's roots are tightly packed in a container, usually going in a circular pattern around the pot. The plant is suffering from neglect—not enough nutrients, air, or water. It definitely needs repotting. The tangled knot of roots can stress the plant. The family situation can be salvaged by reconnecting, making some goals, and finding what satisfies them.

To fix a root-bound plant, you need to take it out of its current ill-fitting pot, loosen the roots, and put it in a bigger pot that is at least two inches bigger, with plenty of fresh soil. It must get the right nutrients, as well as water, and either sun or shade or a combination. Compare that now to the family experiencing the blahs. Loosening the tangled roots is like unlocking the family from indifference. Putting the plant into a bigger pot is like expanding one's horizons from funk to fun. Fresh soil, nutrients, and water are compared to attending to the needs of the family, individually and as a unit. Being in the sun or shade will cause one to thrive, as it is in its proper element. Adding fertilizer will contribute to healthy and vigorous growth. All families, like plants, need to grow and bloom. If you don't have the right nutrients, you will have dull-looking plants that have weak stems and a lack of color. Maybe start with a slow-release fertilizer at first to see how it goes with everyone. You don't want yourself or anyone feeling overwhelmed.

Nobody can be hard on the Rootbound family, as we can all relate at some conjuncture. All of a sudden change happened and continued to happen, and the family got out of sync. Some of the changes could be the kids went off to college, got married, or the family was not a nuclear family due to divorce or death. My children are spaced four and five years apart, and occasionally it was challenging to find something to do that interested all three of them.

Somewhere along the line, people in a rut stopped acting like a family, like the plant that got forgotten because there was work, children's activities, care or visits to elderly family, and a host of things that took priority. That rootbound plant just needed a bit of attention. It needed more room, nutrients, water, and fertilizer. Romina needed to be listened to about her friend troubles and her waning self-image. Rory's grades were slipping. He wanted someone to play hoops with him, but everyone was disinterested or tired, so after a few requests, he stopped asking. The husband and wife just unintentionally took each other for granted. Sounds like fresh soil and nutrients are needed, and communication and care would be a good start.

This is about getting back your mojo with yourself and with

each other; you know feeling good and functioning well and that you have purpose and are experiencing positive relationships. Many partners that have been together for a while stop telling each other "I love you" and stop giving compliments. Consider restarting those lovely verbal sentiments. Helping each other with chores shows partnership. My husband starts the tea kettle for me daily just to be nice. I will bring him water when he does the yard, which shows that I care he stays hydrated. He brings me something I like from the grocery store. We have our prayer chairs, so we make this habit of praying a priority. Sometimes it has slipped for us to go and have fun, so in this area one must be intentional.

Skills to try:

1. Forget blaming and just acknowledge the rut and begin the process to improve the situation. You can only change yourself. If you know the area that caused the rut, then start there.

2. Do you need purpose? Plan goals and include vacations. If no vacations can be planned, then plan weekends where life allows some growth and fun. If you can't plan weekends, then plan evenings. Without some variety, then a rut is easy to get into and stay in.

3. Try something new. Get the fun and spark back. That will look different to different people. To one that may mean being spontaneous, and to another that may mean saying yes to family bowling or a bike ride. But by all means, communicate a plan via a family meeting as to what each would like and, at other times, make it a surprise. Like the slow-release fertilizer, it's about adding it, getting started, and taking small steps like a walk, a game night, or going to the beach.

4. Look at your repotted plant (family) in a few weeks and see if it perked up—if it has a brighter color with new leaf growth. Do some self-discovery as to what you need to bring joy back.

5. Friends and family who have known you pretty well can be consulted as to what they see that is keeping you stuck in an old pot. Ask them to be honest with their insight, such as where they see you are stressed, unhappy, or unmotivated and a suggestion to fix it so you can move forward.

6. Put it all to prayer. The Lord has the best ideas. He is big with rejuvenation, plant or person.

Psalm 119:37a (NIV), "Turn my eyes away from worthless things."

The request from this psalmist to the Lord is to not allow what has no value to affect his inner walk with the Lord. He does not want to be led astray.

Response:

_____

_____

_____

_____

_____

_____

_____

_____

_____

_____

_____

_____

_____

_____

_____

_____

_____

_____

_____

Laugh and Be Silly

As you are right near the end of your journey with learning and applying new coping skills, I want to close with something funny. Try this cute little joke on for size:

A man and his wife are awakened at three in the morning by a loud pounding on the door. The man gets up and opens the door to find a groggy stranger who asks for a push. The man annoyingly states, "No, it's three in the morning, and it's pouring rain," and he goes back to bed. The man tells his wife about the man at the door who needed a push, but he refused because it was late and raining hard. The wife reminds her husband that a few months ago when they broke down and needed a push, a stranger helped them. So the man gets up, dresses, and goes out in the pouring rain to find the stranger. He calls out, "Are you still here?" The stranger responds, "Yes." "Do you still need a push?" "Yes, please," says the man. "Okay, I will help you. Where are you?" The stranger responds, "I'm over here on the swing."

If you got a chuckle out of the silliness, then you benefitted your mental health. Newport Academy wrote the following on the mental health benefits of laughter:

> *Releases endorphins: Natural chemicals in the body, endorphins promote a sense of well-being and stress relieve.*
>
> *Decreases anger: When we're in a difficult situation or in a disagreement with another person, seeing the humor in it can help. Specifically, laughter defuses anger, conflict and self-blame.*
>
> *Eases distressing emotions: Laughter counteracts feelings of anxiety and sadness. Moreover, it helps us*

release other intense emotions, such as grief.

Relaxes and revitalizes: Along with reducing stress, laughter also increases our energy levels. Therefore, we stay focused more easily.

Changes your perspective: Laughter helps us access another point of view. We begin to see something in a new, less scary way when we can laugh about it. In addition, humor helps us take things less seriously.

Reduces stress: when we laugh and smile, cortisol levels decrease. Cortisol is the stress hormone, so lower levels are better for our mental health. Laughter increases our stress resilience.

Brings more joy and fun into our life: This is self-explanatory.

Go ahead—giggle, laugh, or roar, and you guarantee a plus for your mental health. Sometimes you can even laugh so hard you cry. Laughter is a good painkiller. The more you laugh and look at life positively, the less chance you have of developing a chronic ailment; thus, it improves your resistance to disease. It releases oxygen to the heart, lungs, and muscles. For those days we have brain fog, a good laugh would put humor in our brain instead of tension. It helps squash the inner critic as well.

And finally, these typos from some church ladies who forgot to use spell check:

"The peacemaking meeting scheduled for today has been canceled due to a conflict."

"Remember in prayer the many who are sick of our community."

"For those of you who have children and don't know it, we have a nursery downstairs."

Skills to try:

1. Obviously look for something funny to read, watch, or listen to. Make this a regular thing you do. It is virtually a guarantee it will lighten up your mood.

2. Spend time with people with a good sense of humor.

3. Listen to people laugh. There is something contagious about it.

4. Increasing your silliness will decrease how serious life has hit you. If you are a very serious person with tough life circumstances happening now, make the effort even if it feels odd.

5. Do something silly. Life is short; start enjoying it. How about skipping, dancing wildly, talking funny, applying social media filters, or throwing food at a friend? Karaoke anyone?

6. Put out the stop sign to Bleak Blair and Poppy Pooh Pah. Negative people will discourage you in your journey to be happier and to be laughing more. They drain your growing good mood.

Psalm 126:2 (NIV), "Our mouths were filled with laughter, our tongues with songs of joy. Then it was said among the nations; 'The Lord has done great things for them. The Lord has done great things for us, and we are filled with joy.'"

Let that laughter not be contained.

Response:

_____

_____

_____

_____

_____

_____

_____

_____

_____

_____

_____

_____

_____

_____

_____

_____

_____

_____

Desiderata

I found this poem hanging on a church wall in Amherst, Nova Scotia. I was twelve at the time, and it made such an impression as I read the wisdom and felt peace in it. I found twenty-three coping skills, maybe more, as it depends on one's interpretation.

Go placidly amid the noise and the haste and remember what peace there may be in silence. As far as possible, without surrender, be on good terms with all persons.

Speak your truth quietly and clearly; and listen to others, even to the dull and ignorant; they too have their story.

Avoid loud and aggressive persons; they are vexatious to the spirit. If you compare yourself with others, you may become vain or bitter, for always there will be greater and lesser persons than yourself.

Enjoy your achievements as well as your plans. Keep interested in your own career, however humble; it is a real possession in the changing fortunes of time.

Exercise caution in your business affairs, for the world is full of trickery. But let this not blind you to what virtue there is; many persons strive for high ideals, and everywhere life is full of heroism.

Be yourself. Especially do not feign affection. Neither be cynical about love; for in the face of all aridity and disenchantment, it is perennial as the grass.

Take kindly the counsel of the years, gracefully surrendering the things of youth. Nurture strength of spirit to shield you in sudden misfortune. But do not distress yourself with dark imaginings. Many fears are born of fatigue and loneliness.

Beyond a wholesome discipline, be gentle with your-self. You are a child of the universe no less than the trees and the stars; you have a right to be here.

And whether or not it is clear to you, no doubt the universe is unfolding as it should. Therefore, be at peace with God, whatever you conceive him to be. And whatever your labors and aspirations, in the noisy confusion of life, keep peace in your soul. With all its sham, drudgery and broken dreams, it is still a beautiful world. Be cheerful. Strive to be happy.

Max Ehrmann 1927

Skill to try:

1. Enjoy this and take it in slowly. Read again and pick out the coping skills. Are there any you want to apply?

Ecclesiastes 3:1a (NIV), "There is a time for everything, and a season for every activity under heaven."

God is sovereign over all creation and time. There is a proper time for everything.

Response:

_____

_____

_____

_____

_____

_____

_____

_____

_____

_____

_____

_____

_____

_____

_____

_____

_____

_____

_____

_____

_____

Dear reader,

I trust you benefitted from the stories and skills offered in this book and you will continue to reap good things as a result. May God bless you with His highest and best in all your endeavors!

If you'd like, you can check out my website **patriciatilley.com**.

Patricia I. Tilley, LMHC

Disclaimer:

No skills in this book should be used as a substitute for advice from your doctor or another qualified clinician.

CPSIA information can be obtained
at www.ICGtesting.com
Printed in the USA
BVHW042026150223
658591BV00013B/446